JOBSEARCH

JOBSEARCH

THE COMPLETE MANUAL FOR JOBSEEKERS

H. LEE RUST
edited by Joyce Benington

amacom

A DIVISION OF AMERICAN MANAGEMENT ASSOCIATIONS

80- 42892

Library of Congress Cataloging in Publication Data

Rust, H   Lee.
  Jobsearch: the complete manual for jobseekers.

  Includes index.
  1. Vocational guidance. I. Benington, Joyce.
II. Title.
HF5381.R79   650'.14   78-24184
ISBN 0-8144-5501-8

Second Printing

FOREWORD

You want to find a new job. How should you go about it? Write a resume? Contact a few friends? Answer some help wanted ads?

Don't.

You can't afford to let your search be a haphazard effort. After all, the job you find may absorb 15 years of your career. It will provide the livelihood for your family and will occupy the majority of your waking hours. It can be a satisfying, challenging experience, or it can be total drudgery in an incompatible environment. It can advance your career or stunt it.

Your next job may be the most important move in your professional life. To find it you should use an efficient, systematic career marketing plan. This is jobsearch, the program presented in this manual. It prepares you step by step to market yourself to those employers, and only those, who meet your career needs. Neither your time nor your energy will be wasted on ineffective methods. You will avoid mistakes that can impede your search and cause you to miss opportunities.

Each task, from defining your market to negotiating your salary, is explained completely. All contingencies for your job campaign are covered. Examples show you how others have solved problems, located job leads, and sold themselves in situations similar to your own. The labyrinth we call "The Job Market" is divided into its component parts with concise techniques developed to penetrate each.

Although the names and addresses have been disguised, the experiences and people described in this book are real. They had problems or fears similar to those you may feel as you approach the job market. They used the jobsearch methods presented in this manual to overcome these fears and problems and go on to advance or reestablish their careers in new positions with new companies.

You can find the job you want quickly and efficiently. But you must remember—

Jobs do not always go to the most qualified candidate.

They go to the candidate who sells himself or herself the best.

This jobsearch manual will show you how to be this successful candidate.

CONTENTS

PART TWO

MARKETING

PART THREE

SELLING YOURSELF

PART ONE

STARTING YOUR JOBSEARCH

CHAPTER 1

INTRODUCTION AND
INSTRUCTIONS

An executive came to my office not long ago to discuss his career. David was with a well-known electric switch-gear manufacturer. His position was secure; he had been with the company for 17 years, rising to become manager of two plants with 300 employees each. But he was uncomfortable with his career and his future. At age 52 he felt that his job progress should not slow down. In fact, he felt more prepared to take advantage of his experience than at any previous time. Still, he had not been able to move beyond plant operations—larger plants, yes; new locations, yes. But the promotion that would put him in a position to affect the future direction of the company remained elusive. It was obvious he needed to make a change. He needed to put his career back into his own hands.

At that time I ran a service company to help executives like David. To be precise, I was helping business people sell themselves. I was good at it primarily because I realized years ago that three aspects of selling people are of paramount importance. One, experienced individuals have within themselves and their backgrounds a product to sell; two, the methods used to package and present this product in the job market affect its acceptance; and three, most business people are ill equipped to make this sale, although it is frequently the most important sale of their careers.

Why should even a seasoned executive know how to find a job? Often his or her experience at job seeking is no broader than that of someone entering the job market for the first time. During 30 years of experience with only three job changes, David had never been required to plan and execute a marketing campaign to sell himself. Even though he had hired others, he actually knew little about the job market.

How and when do companies identify high-level personnel needs? How do they screen and hire management employees? Of perhaps greater importance, how do they eliminate the candidates who are not hired? What is the function of the resume in this entire process? How and to whom does the job candidate address himself?

Through my firm, JOBSEARCH, we helped David answer not only these but numerous other questions. We also showed him how to organize and execute a complete marketing campaign for that difficult product—himself.

We told him, however, that the sale would not be an easy one to make. We explained that it could not be the desultory effort it often is with too many executives. It had to be both planned and thorough. We further pointed out that to make the sale his campaign would also have to be massive. It worked. David is now the vice-president of operations for one of the largest specialty steel product fabricators in the United States.

It can also work for you. If you have already attained a management role or if you have educated yourself with both instruction and experience to accept such a role, you can benefit from the jobsearch program presented in this manual.

But why should you do it? Why should you expend the time and considerable effort required to analyze your market, package your product, advertise its availability, and make the sale? Perhaps you are like David, secure in your job, satisfied with your past accomplishments, but uneasy about your immediate or long-range prospects. Career advancement demands change. After you have mastered a task or made your maximum contribution to a position, you must decide whether to stay or move. If the appropriate move can be made within your present company, fine; do it. If it cannot, the decision—although it may be more difficult—must still be made.

A change in companies may require moving your family. It will certainly include the risks of an unknown environment with new colleagues, new superiors, and new problems. But you must realize that it will do little for your career to have five years' experience twice, even less to have one year's experience five times. Your career belongs only to you. You must guide and develop it yourself. If it becomes stagnant, staying where you are is no less a decision—even if it is not a conscious one—than deciding to make a move. Too often the refusal to make this decision turns out to be the wrong decision.

There are many other reasons to seek new employment. At JOB-SEARCH we worked with men and women who had a variety of motivational needs and goals. We helped those who primarily were seeking increase in compensation, often substantial. Persons desiring to move to another city or preferred area successfully used our program, as well as those who wanted to avoid a transfer. We executed campaigns for career changes from one industry to another, from the military to business, and from private to public service employment. In most cases, prior to these changes the men and women were adequately paid, made contributions to their organizations, and were reasonably content. But they realized that something was missing. Adequate compensation and moderate satisfaction with their work was not enough. Call it new challenge, a chance to improve either pay or environment, the prospect of better use of their skills—in any event, it meant a job change. Invariably the change was warranted; they and their careers benefited. Most executives do not change jobs too frequently; they change too seldom. David, for instance, should have made his decision five years earlier.

You may not be in this situation. The decision may have been made for you. Perhaps you were fired or laid off or retired too early. Now a jobsearch is inevitable. It should not, however, be executed with any less precision; nor need it be any less successful.

For whatever reason, your decision is made. You are ready to apply your experience and efforts to the exciting, although perhaps initially forbidding, business area we call "The Job Market." This manual will show you how. In these first pages you are starting a job that will be one of the most absorbing and interesting experiences of your entire career. This is the job of finding a new position, a new employer, and a new opportunity.

Let me assure you, somewhere there is a company that can use your talent and experience and pay you well for them. Not only that, it is probably located where you want to live. Your job is to find that company and sell yourself into the position you want. It can be done—more easily than you think. I have done it too many times to think otherwise, and I have done it with the techniques set out in this book.

This jobsearch manual offers a complete, programmed approach to the job-seeking process. It was developed over a four-year period by helping individuals like you find the employment of their choice. Virtually all approaches to the job market were tried, modified, and tried again. Records were kept to determine the most effective methods of obtaining job interviews and, through these interviews, securing job offers. Ineffective methods were modified and in some cases were dropped entirely. In addition, a review of available literature on the job market and the job-seeking process was used to evaluate the jobsearch method against the approach and suggestions from other knowledgeable sources. Used with care and judgment, it can help you reach your immediate and long-range career goals.

But how long will it take? This is one of the questions I'm asked most frequently. There is no average time. At JOBSEARCH we had clients who used our interview techniques and secured a new position in less than a week with a prospect they had in hand. In most cases, however, you should count on an effort that will absorb between one to four months. Among other factors beyond your control, it will depend on the time you can devote to the search — whether you are employed and can work on the search only at night and on weekends or whether you can devote full time to your campaign.

What will it cost? The expenses associated with supplies, postage, secretarial and autotyping services, long-distance telephone calls, and miscellaneous items usually run between two hundred and three hundred dollars. This depends, of course, on the extent of the search, on whether it is local or national. In any case, it is a small investment in your future. This book is not designed for the college graduate looking for his or her first job. It is for the person who needs to advance his or her career with a strategically chosen move and understands the value of the required investment in time and money.

HOW TO USE THIS MANUAL

The jobsearch method is set out in chronological sequence. It should be followed in the order in which it is presented. Do not try one section and then another. Instead, schedule your work to produce the maximum number of interviews within a relatively short period of time. Your objective is to secure multiple job offers that can then be compared and negotiated one against the others.

You should remember, however, that seeking a new position is a personal endeavor. Your immediate situation, your experience, and your background are different from those of all other individuals. For this reason you may find it appropriate to put additional emphasis on one or more marketing techniques, perhaps neglecting others entirely. Use your own judgment in tailoring the program to your maximum advantage.

Before starting any actual work, look through the entire manual; review the table of contents in detail, and study the forms and examples in the Jobsearch Workbook at the end of this manual. Familiarize yourself with the information included, the forms you will complete, and the marketing techniques suggested. This will give you an overview of the jobsearch approach.

Then establish a preliminary schedule of work to be accomplished and milestones to be reached. A form (#1) is included in the workbook section to record this projected work schedule. Once having established it, make every effort to adhere to your timetable. Be realistic but also demand the most of yourself. The best results will be obtained with a smooth, continuous effort directed toward a specific time goal.

As you proceed through the manual, or when circumstances change, your schedule should be updated. In this way you will be continually working toward realistic goals.

Discipline yourself to meet your goals. Establish a certain period each day, or certain time segments during each week, to work on your jobsearch campaign. If you are unemployed, approach your campaign as you would a full-time job. Start at eight o'clock each morning; work five or six hours a day, five days a week. During most of your search there will be sufficient work to absorb this time. And much of the work will be both interesting and stimulating.

A specific area, usually in your home, to be used as your jobsearch office, will prove advantageous in conducting your search. This space should include a desk or a table that can serve as a desk, a telephone, and a place to keep stationery, reference books, and other supplies. Conduct the search from this office as you would any other well-organized marketing or sales campaign. Information must be readily available as you contact prospective employers or as they contact you—frequently when you least expect it.

You will find a standard three-ring binder most effective as a master file for your correspondence, contact lists, and other jobsearch information. Buy tabbed dividers and label them: To Do, Resume and Data, Personal Contacts, Ad Answers, Mail Campaign, Other Contacts, Prospects, and Miscellaneous. Filing your work in appropriate sections in this notebook will facilitate your locating them when they are needed.

In the "To Do" section, add a blank page of lined paper. This will be used for listing work to be accomplished or required follow-up during the current week. As items are completed they should be marked off, with new items added to the bottom of the list. At the beginning of each week, the list should be rewritten and the old one discarded.

A successful jobsearch effort is largely determined by attention to numerous details. This requires organization. In your correspondence, personal contacts, and follow-up with potential employers, you will be at least partially judged by your ability to organize your work. A well-organized, well-executed jobsearch will be evident to prospective employers and will act in your favor.

EXPENSE RECORDS.   DEDUCTION FOR FEDERAL INCOME TAX.   In 1975 the Internal Revenue Service (IRS) changed its former practice and began to allow expenses associated with a search for employment as deductions for federal income tax purposes. Deductible items include all expenses incurred as a result of the search, including fees paid to an agency or consultant, whether successful or not. Travel expenses are also included if the primary purpose of the trip is to secure a new job.

Expenses are not deductible for a person seeking his or her first job or for individuals who have been unemployed long enough to create a substantial lack of continuity between jobs. Neither are they deductible for a search directed toward a different trade or business from that practiced previously.

In determining the deductibility in your own case, do not necessarily consider a career change as a change of trade or business as defined by the IRS. If you are a manager and are seeking a job as a manager or executive, this is not a change of trade or business even though you might change industries or the type of business. If you are currently in sales, any new job involving sales or taking advantage of your sales experience will most likely be recognized as being in the same trade or business. If you have questions concerning your own case, ask a certified public accountant or qualified lawyer for his or her advice or opinion.

In order to obtain your income tax deduction, your expense records must be complete and detailed. You must be able to substantiate them if you are audited by the Internal Revenue Service. This means that you should keep all receipts or other information which supports your expense records.

See forms #2–#5 in the workbook section for recording your automobile, telephone, and traveling expenses as well as a summary record for these and miscellaneous items. Record all your expenses as they occur. Include automobile travel even for short local trips. This expense can accumulate and represent a substantial amount during your entire job campaign. Record telephone calls as they are made including date, city, and person called. When your monthly bill arrives, fill in the toll charges, add 10 percent for tax and service, and transfer the total to the summary page. Use copies of the Travel Expense Report for trips that are not company reimbursed or for submission to companies that do not give you their own form.

OBJECTIVES AND APPROACH

The largest employer in the United States is private industry. Most individuals seek jobs in this sector of our economy. For this reason the major emphasis of this jobsearch manual is on jobs in the business world. This does not mean the program cannot be used with equal facility and success to secure jobs with associations, nonprofit institutions, professional groups, or government agencies. In fact, even with a former career in business you might wish to target a portion of your jobsearch effort toward one or more of these other potential areas of employment. In such cases, use care to modify your correspondence and other information to conform to the requirements, objectives, and — in some instances — jargon of these groups.

One of our most successful searches was done with a career army officer who wanted to enter private business. It was difficult for him to drop 20 years of military language and tailor his resume and letters to the business world. He did it well, however, and is now personnel director in a 500-employee company. It is not the 7,000-person military installation for which he performed similar functions, but the pay is substantially higher and opportunity is unlimited. He gained the control over his career that he wanted.

As you proceed through this jobsearch manual, be cognizant of the objectives of each section of work. The overall program is designed not simply to find a job but to secure for you a career position that will offer maximum compensation and job satisfaction. This dictates a multifaceted and thorough approach to the job market. By pursuing effective marketing techniques simultaneously, you can attract a number of job offers at about the same time. Success in this effort will give you the luxury of choosing among available alternatives, of using one offer as a negotiating tool with others, and of planning your future career utilizing all available options.

In Part One of this manual, your objective is to gather information and establish the basis for the correspondence you will need in your marketing effort. Although important, this work is preparatory only. You will not receive a job offer in response to a letter or a resume. An offer will be received only through a personal interview. You must sell yourself to an employer face to face.

With this in mind, the objective of the marketing phase of this jobsearch manual — Part Two — is to secure the maximum number of personal contacts with prospective employers: to maximize interviews. During the selling phase of job interviews and the follow-up described in Part Three, the objective is directed toward attracting job offers that will give you the necessary choices to guide your future career.

THE JOB MARKET AND YOU

In seeking a new position you should not be concerned about the state of the economy or any comments you might read or hear concerning the availability of jobs in your field. Whether the country is in expansion or recession — whether you are looking in a broad or a narrow field — attractive jobs are available. These are created by the mobility of the workforce; the death, retirement, and promotion of current job holders; and the growth of companies throughout the economy. Your basic approach to the job market will not be altered by these factors of supply and demand. Although they may influence the extent of your search or the emphasis placed on various marketing methods, the techniques are the same.

Just remember that regardless of prevailing economic conditions, good jobs are still available. The jobsearch method will help you identify these positions and direct your efforts to a successful conclusion.

WHAT EMPLOYERS ARE LOOKING FOR.   Most resumes are a litany of job titles and responsibilities. They are written as a career history of the candidate. They should be written instead as a sales tool directed toward the expected audience. A company will seldom hire you because of titles you held or responsibilities you exercised. They are interested in your ability to produce profits or to improve the efficiency of their organization.

A company either makes a profit or dies. If a firm hires you for $20,000 per year, they expect a $40,000 return. It is obviously a losing game to hire you at that salary and get a $15,000 return.

Your ability to make such a contribution can best be determined by those of your past accomplishments that relate to the profit or success of your former employer. For this reason this jobsearch manual is accomplishments oriented.

As you proceed through the manual, never lose sight of the fact that you are hired to produce profits or efficiencies and usually for no other reason. Although different words are used to describe profits, this is as true for a charitable or social service organization as for a business venture. While your career goals, job satisfaction, and personal fulfillment are important to you, they are of no importance to a prospective employer. It is up to you, not the prospective employer, to determine that your job and career offer personal satisfaction.

It is irritating to most business executives to receive a resume that starts with a job objective stating, "I seek a management-level position affording the opportunity to broaden my background and experience while offering the potential for growth and compensation commensurate with my abilities in a self-satisfying career."

That is a quote from a resume in my JOBSEARCH files. The client quickly agreed that he did not need any of these self-gratifying platitudes. Once he analyzed his past accomplishments, he realized he had the wherewithal to sell himself into a position that would give him the job excitement and pay he wanted. And he went on to do it with no reference to such an objective.

SEARCH WHILE EMPLOYED OR UNEMPLOYED.   A popular misconception about jobs and the job market is that it is easier to get a job when you have a job. This is simply not true. It is based on the belief that when you are employed there is no need to explain why you left your former position. It fails to take into consideration that a similar explanation may be required for all previous job changes.

No job candidate offers ideal qualifications for any position. Explanation is a part of the history of your entire career. In many cases individuals interviewing you for a new position have been terminated or have made job changes during their careers.

There is, of course, some advantage in having continuing income if you are employed during your search. Nevertheless, most advantages in being employed during the search are compensated for by the time you have to devote to your search if you are not employed. In either case the work is the same, the approach is the same, and the results should not differ.

CONDUCTING AN ANONYMOUS SEARCH.   Steps can be taken to keep your jobsearch campaign confidential if you should find it necessary to do so because of your current employment. In general, this will reduce the response to your campaign. It does not mean, however, that you will be unsuccessful; it means only that your options may be more limited than with an open search.

You must judge the extent to which your anonymity is important. If you are unsuccessful in your first campaign, you will still be gainfully employed. You can wait a few months and begin again. At that time you might reevaluate the importance of confidentiality and its effect on the success of your search.

In only four cases was a JOBSEARCH client's search discovered prematurely. In none of these situations was the person terminated. On the contrary, a mutually agreeable transition period was worked out. As a consequence, these JOBSEARCH clients were then able to concentrate on their future as well as use their employers as references.

In one instance a client answered a blind help wanted advertisement that had been placed by his own company. The requirements specified in the ad matched his target perfectly. He was in pharmaceutical sales with a desire to move into marketing and product management where he could use his chemistry and marketing MBA degrees. He thus secured the job he wanted without changing companies. Carefully assess the need for confidentiality as well as for the job prospects you might find without a move.

If your search is confidential, you will be severely restricted in the use of personal contacts. Rather than broadcasting your availability to all business friends and associates who might help, you will be forced to limit appeals to a select few you can trust implicitly. If your situation is particularly sensitive or you are well known in the area of your search, you may find it necessary to eliminate all personal contacts.

You can, however, conduct an effective direct mail campaign and answer help wanted advertisements by using a close personal friend as an intermediary. This is done by following the same procedures as for the direct mail marketing letter and ad responses described in the appropriate sections of this manual. Instead of using your own name and address on the letterhead, use that of your friend, writing the letters as if they were being written in your behalf.

Look at the sample of a direct mail marketing letter and an ad response (#6, #7) done in this manner. Note that the reason for confidentiality is stated in the letters. Each letter ends with a disclaimer of any economic interest in an eventual agreement between you and a new employer. These are important points. The reason for confidentiality must be plausible. Otherwise it will be viewed as a gimmick and restrict the rate of response even more severely. Because on occasion employment agencies or other "finders" answer help wanted ads or send out letters similar to these, the commission or fee disclaimer is used to advise the reader that no such situation exists.

In this type of search you must use a friend to receive calls and letters at his or her own address and telephone number. Do not attempt the subterfuge of a false name over your own address. This ploy will eventually become known to any respondent and will act to your disfavor. Nor should you use a blind post office box; few companies will respond to an unnamed party. A "Situations Wanted" advertisement, blind or not, is an ineffective method of finding employment. The methods used to protect the confidentiality of your search must be as genuine as the reasons for it.

The choice of an intermediary in a confidential jobsearch campaign is of utmost importance. In many cases, prospective employers will speak to this person first. This conversation will constitute their first evaluation of you even though you are not speaking for yourself.

If possible, your intermediary should be a person familiar with the field in which you seek employment. He or she should be on the same level or above that of the position you seek, and must be conversant with your background, talents, and objectives. A copy of your resume, your accomplishments list, and the mailing list for the letter campaign should be readily available to him or her. For responses to help wanted advertisements, your intermediary should have a copy of the advertisement stapled to the letter you wrote.

Even though these letters will be written, typed, and mailed by you, they should be personally signed by your intermediary. In signing each letter, he or she should check the name to be certain the salutation is appropriate. You might have addressed a letter to Mr. Blakley when your intermediary would have started with "Dear Bill."

Never take undue advantage of your friend during your campaign. All the work involved — including overseeing printing of the letterhead, typing, stuffing envelopes, and mailing letters — should be done by you. As soon as any real interest in you is established, the intermediary should divulge your name, offer to put you in contact with the prospective employer, and withdraw gracefully from any further involvement in interviews or negotiations.

When you consider a confidential search, think carefully about your current situation — the probability of your employer's learning that you are looking and the effect on your job if that should occur. Most business people whom you contact in your search will respect a simple request for confidentiality. In addition, they will want to know who is interested in their firm and the identity of his or her current employer.

An employer who hears that you are interested in changing jobs may still keep you until you have found a new position. This is usually the case if you continue to contribute to the company. After all, your employer needs time to find your replacement. On the other hand, if you are terminated immediately, you will be free to devote all your efforts to finding a new job. After you have definitely decided to make a change, this may not be as bad as it first appears.

In any case, do not use your search as a bargaining tool with your current employer. You may be offered inducements to stay on, but you will have damaged your reputation with the company. Regardless of how attractive the inducements, your future with the firm may be jeopardized. When you are considered for promotions, there will be a lingering doubt about your remaining with the company.

If your search is discovered, discuss it frankly and openly with your employer. Make definite arrangements to complete the tasks you have in process for the company, and offer to help in finding your replacement. You must leave on the best possible terms. Don't forget that a good reference from your employer will be of assistance in your search. But don't bargain to stay. Your decision is made and you must act on it.

IF YOU ARE FIRED

A large number, if not a majority, of business people who have led active careers have been fired or dismissed in some other manner from a company. Although this may create a severe psychological trauma, it is not the end of your career. On the contrary, it can be an exciting opportunity. You will be free to concentrate on finding a new position. There is no reason why this new position should not advance your career. You must put the trauma behind you and get to work on the job at hand.

On losing their jobs, most people think first of taking time off to rest and decide what to do next. This is a mistake. Even a short vacation will cause you to lose momentum. Instead of relaxing and using the time to think constructively about your future, you will worry about your next job—how you are going to find it and whether it will be as good as the one you just lost.

We had JOBSEARCH clients who came to us after such vacations. Invariably, it was more difficult to start a search in these instances. The clients were confused. They felt rejected and could not objectively view their past careers to identify the strengths that were their best sales tools.

You must begin preparing your jobsearch campaign immediately after losing your job. Take a vacation after your campaign has been successfully completed, before you report to your new position.

When you are fired, for whatever reason, your new job starts the moment you are told. You must act in a businesslike manner. Don't become emotional, and don't try to talk your employer into keeping you. It never works. Simply try to determine the reasons the action was taken. It may also be important to give your side of the story just for the record. If this seems advisable, keep it brief. Don't be drawn into an argument. You have another important item to discuss—your severance benefits—and for this you don't want a hostile atmosphere.

Negotiate your severance benefits politely but firmly. These benefits may represent a major portion of your livelihood until you are in your new job. Be realistic, but try to get more than you are initially offered. Don't forget there are numerous benefits other than cash payments. You may find the company is willing to give you free secretarial services during your jobsearch campaign or allow you to use a company car for several weeks. These and similar items can reduce expenses while you are unemployed.

During these conversations, it is also important to determine what your former employer will say about your termination. You must know if you're to be given a poor reference in order to soften its impact when you approach a new company.

In the coming weeks you will have to tell your friends and business acquaintances, as well as potential employers, why you were terminated. You will find it helpful to write a one-paragraph explanation using your own reasons. These may or may not be the same as those given by your employer, but they should be the truth as you see it. Your explanation should contain little negative information—preferably none. Then, once it is written down, don't change your story.

YOUR ATTITUDE

A major obstacle to success in your search for a new job is your fear of being rejected. Particularly in the case of persons who have been fired, their fear of rejection is frequently so great that they subconsciously disqualify themselves before they can be refused. This can best be overcome by conducting a thorough search and uncovering a number of opportunities for consideration. In the process of doing this you must understand the procedures for the sale of any product. Every individual in the potential market does not represent a buyer. Some will neither want nor need the product you sell.

In a jobsearch campaign, you are the product. You are selling your own talent and experience. These may be of great value to one company and of no value whatsoever to another. Rejection is part of making the sale. You want only one job. The market is large. Expect refusals and do not let them affect your determination or your self-confidence.

We had one JOBSEARCH client who frequently canceled job interviews because of conflicts that arose with his duties at the time. Another invariably showed up late for interviews although he was habitually punctual. In both cases these clients were seeking ready excuses for the refusals they feared. Once they understood what they were doing and the reasons for their actions, they went on to secure the jobs they wanted.

Your attitude about yourself and your objectives is important to the success of your campaign. Written and verbal communications should be positive and direct in tone. You should feel self-assured, comfortable with your past accomplishments, and confident about the future.

If these are not your current attitudes, they will change as you progress through this manual. The more you work on your future career, the more contacts you make, the more interviews you have, the more convinced you will become of your probable success.

Your best job interviews will be those you do not consider crucial. Knowing you have other options, you will be more at ease. This will be evident to the prospective employer and will work to your advantage.

You would not purchase a product in a torn, dirty, or unattractive package. Now you must package yourself for maximum appeal to your potential job market. Your attitude, as well as your personal dress and appearance, is part of this package. Keep it positive and self-assured.

PROFESSIONAL ASSISTANCE

A number of firms, primarily in the five or six largest U.S. cities, offer assistance to persons seeking employment. Although this jobsearch manual is designed to eliminate the need for such assistance, it is advisable to understand what is available. In some instances a job seeker may wish to consider some sort of specialized help.

Firms that work with job seekers are of three basic types — resume services, career counselors, and placement consultants. Of these, the professional resume services should be avoided by virtually all job seekers. Most of these service companies offer a standard resume form that lists a candidate's past job titles and responsibilities. Costs range from $25 to $1,000. Not only do these resumes neglect the important emphasis on accomplishments, which are the candidate's major selling points, but they are also easily recognizable by most company executives with experience in the job market. A company expects your presentation to be your own. If it is not, it will tend to discredit you. In addition, many of the resume services urge the candidate to have his or her resume printed in large quantities and offer to mail them out to a standard list of company presidents. This jobsearch manual will explain why these suggestions are erroneous and will give you effective alternatives.

Generally, career counselors should also be avoided. They are expensive and are not needed by most experienced business people. Typical charges range from $1,500 to $4,000. For these fees the job seeker receives a battery of psychological and vocational tests coupled with counseling to help in patterning future career objectives. This may be followed by some help in turning these objectives into a job. If they have a well-planned jobsearch campaign, most business people can do better executing it themselves.

If, however, you feel you need professional guidance in making your immediate and long-term vocational choices, consider consulting a good industrial psychologist. For fees ranging from $200 to $500 these professionals will offer the same type of testing and evaluation as the heavily advertised career counseling firms. Most such individuals or firms are listed in the Yellow Pages of major city telephone directories. Directors of personnel of large corporations can also recommend industrial psychologists whom they use in candidate screening processes.

Placement consultants usually offer a combination of career counseling and help in securing employment with major emphasis on the candidate's jobsearch. Again these services are expensive in relation to the assistance provided. Fees range from $2,500 to 10 or 15 percent of the candidate's first year's salary. Although these firms relieve the candidate of the major portion of work involved in the search, their efficiency and methods are difficult — if not impossible — to judge prior to entering into a binding contract. Because a jobsearch is a close, personal endeavor, job seekers will find they can do a better job of choosing target companies and presenting themselves than a third party who knows them only superficially.

CHAPTER 2

PRELIMINARY WORK

This jobsearch manual is directed toward four major and a number of minor approaches to the job market. These various methods are composed of numerous small details that will require your attention. Your campaign is a business venture. You will need organization, supplies, and services in order to conduct the venture successfully. Prior to actually working on your campaign, complete, or at least start, all the preliminary work discussed in this chapter. You will then be assured that items you need are available at the appropriate time and that your search can proceed smoothly from this point to its successful conclusion.

ORGANIZE YOUR EFFORT

Again, organize your effort. Set up a jobsearch office. File materials in your notebook; do not let unfiled materials accumulate. Record on your "To Do" list all work and follow-up to be accomplished. Then strike off these items when they have been completed. Schedule time each day or week to devote to your jobsearch effort.

The ability to organize your effort will have a marked influence on the success of your campaign.

PERSONAL STATIONERY

For your jobsearch correspondence, you will need personal stationery. Even if you now have stationery, it is probably not adequate for this use. You are conducting a business campaign. You should use stationery printed in a business style and format.

It should be on a good grade of white paper, 8½ × 11 inches with matching envelopes. A 20-pound, 25 percent rag paper will offer the best appearance without excessive expense. Your name and complete address, along with your telephone number, should be printed in block letters centered at the top of the page. Use only one type style for the entire heading. Do not use a print style that is too bold or too elaborate (#8 is a sample of this type of stationery). You may have the heading engraved, but it is more expensive than printing. It may also appear ostentatious and should therefore not be used when seeking a job below $30,000 per year. In most cases, 500 first sheets, 500 envelopes, and 100 blank second sheets will be adequate.

Get two or three quotations on the stationery from local printing companies. Frequently, quick-copy shops specialize in this type of small-order printing and will offer an attractive price. Printing the stationery should not take more than two weeks. Be sure you have a firm deadline from the printer at the time of order. About a week after the order is placed, call to expedite completion. This quantity and style of stationery should cost less than $50.

PHOTOGRAPH

Although you will make limited use of the resume in your jobsearch campaign, you will need one that is well written and well presented. To the extent possible, this resume should show you as a real person. One way to further this objective is to include on the resume a recent photograph of yourself. Even though it is now illegal under equal opportunity laws for a prospective employer to request a photograph, it is not illegal for you to include one unsolicited.

Because of the time required to locate the least expensive source for these photographs and have them made, this detail should be taken care of at the same time you order your stationery. The photograph should be a glossy print, approximately 2 × 2½ inches, showing a head and shoulders view. A man should wear a dark business suit, white shirt, and conservative tie. For a woman, a tailored suit and a conservative blouse are appropriate. Your hair and general appearance should be neat. Take care that the photograph does not make you appear too young or old, sleepy, inattentive, frivolous, or otherwise unbusinesslike.

You will need approximately 25 copies. Most commercial portrait studios are not equipped to do small multiple copies and will therefore be excessively expensive. This should not be an amateur job, however, unless the amateur chosen has substantial portrait experience. As a source for these photos you might try passport photo shops or discount stores offering children's photographs. Or contact the placement office of a local university. It frequently knows of persons who do resume photographs for graduating seniors. You should be able to purchase these pictures for a dollar each or less.

ESTABLISH INFORMATION SOURCES

Throughout your jobsearch you will need substantial information concerning prospective employers. In the marketing phase of your campaign this will consist primarily of names and addresses of companies that might be of potential interest to you. This information must also contain the names of individuals in these companies who would be appropriate recipients of your correspondence.

Much of this information will be available to you locally, particularly if you are conducting a jobsearch campaign limited to your current home area. In most cases, however, some of this information must be ordered. For this reason review all available sources of information at this time, and make a list of those that appear most appropriate to your search. Order immediately by telephone or letter those that must be sent to you.

The following sources of information will be helpful:

Your local library. Most public libraries, in particular the main branch of libraries in major cities, contain extensive sources of business information. This manual includes a list (#9) of business reference books available at large libraries. Visit your local library and discuss your jobsearch campaign with the head of the business or research section. Determine which books on the above-mentioned list are available. Look up other books and directories suggested by your librarian. Study the table of contents of each, and familiarize yourself with the method of listing and the extent and layout of information. In general, these major reference books are too expensive to order specifically for your job campaign. They will, however, include listings of trade periodicals, specialized directories, and association publications that you might wish to order.

The chamber of commerce. Most state chambers of commerce publish directories of industrial and other business firms for their entire state. These directories list companies alphabetically, geographically, and by product or Standard Industrial Classification (SIC) code numbers. Many city chambers of commerce publish similar directories for their Standard Metropolitan Statistical Areas (SMSA) and also have information available concerning local banks, wholesalers, community organizations, distributors, insurance companies, and large employers. If you are conducting a campaign on a local level, or are specifically interested in working in certain states or cities, these directories are excellent sources of information. You can buy them at your local chamber of commerce office or order them by phone or letter. Expect to pay $20 to $30 for most state industrial directories and somewhat less for local directories.

State agencies. Industrial directories are also frequently published by state development, economic, or commerce departments. Call these organizations in states of interest to you. Ascertain the information they have available and its cost. When ordering these directories, be careful not to duplicate information available from the chamber of commerce.

Trade journals. Most trade journals or magazines contain classified help wanted sections. For a search directed toward one or more specific industries, these are better sources of potential job information than the more general classified sections of city newspapers. *Ulrich's International Periodical Directory* and the *Encyclopedia of Business Information Sources* both list trade periodicals. These directories are available in most large libraries. Trade journals exist for almost every conceivable business. Determine which of these magazines might be of assistance in your campaign, and call or write to the publishers to request subscription information and cost. Also request a sample copy. If you subscribe, ask that you be sent the two editions previous to your subscription date.

Association publications. Many trade associations publish newsletters or magazines that have help wanted listings. They also have membership lists that can be excellent sources of information about potential contacts. Look in the Gale Research Company *Encyclopedia of Associations,* also available at large libraries, to determine which of these organizations might be helpful to you. Call them; explain your needs and find out what information they have available that would be useful.

Local newspapers. City newspapers contain more classified job listings than any other single source. Most employment agencies advertise in their local newspaper to fill positions for companies that have retained them. In addition, local businesses use classified newspaper ads to find lower-level or technical employees. Although help wanted ads in city newspapers are more effective as sources of these lower-level jobs, any job seeker interested in a specific city should review the local paper's help wanted advertisements, particularly the Sunday edition. Even if you are conducting the bulk of your campaign in a broader area, subscribe to the Sunday edition of the two or three largest newspapers in that area.

Major city newspapers. Although most city classifieds have only local area listings, there are some exceptions. The six newspapers listed below, all with Sunday circulation of over 600,000, attract help wanted advertising from their entire region of the United States. They also draw advertising for higher-paid positions than those carried in smaller newspapers. If appropriate to your search, subscribe to the Sunday edition of one or more of these newspapers. In general, paying extra for first class mail delivery is not warranted. With normal delivery you will have sufficient time to submit your response. In the list below, the telephone number following the address is that of the circulation or subscription department of the newspaper.

Los Angeles Times
Times-Mirror Square
Los Angeles, California 90053
    Telephone (213) 626-2323

San Francisco Examiner & Chronicle
925 Mission Street
San Francisco, California 94103
    Telephone (415) 777-7000 or 777-7800

Washington Post
1515 L Street, N.W.
Washington, D.C. 20005
    Telephone (202) 223-6100

Chicago Tribune
435 North Michigan Avenue
Chicago, Illinois 60611
    Telephone (312) 222-4100

The New York Times
229 West 43rd Street
New York, New York 10036
    Telephone (212) 556-7292

Atlanta Journal-Constitution
72 Marietta Street, N.W.
Atlanta, Georgia 30383
    Telephone (404) 522-4141

The Wall Street Journal. A nationally distributed business newspaper, *The Wall Street Journal* is probably the best single source of classified help wanted ads for middle- and upper-level positions in all fields. It is appropriate, however, only if you are willing to relocate. It can be purchased daily at most large newsstands. Help wanted advertisements are published primarily on Tuesday and Wednesday. Because *The Wall Street Journal* is printed in four regional editions, be sure you subscribe to and receive the edition for the area in which you wish to conduct your search. The regional editions are Eastern, Midwestern, Southwestern, and Western. Their subscription address is:

The Wall Street Journal
200 Burnett Road
Chicopee, Massachusetts 01021
Telephone (413) 592-7761

College placement publications. Some college placement offices publish lists of available jobs that have been brought to their attention. These lists are sent to their alumni on request and, in some cases, to local residents who did not graduate from the college. To determine if such publications exist and are appropriate to your search, contact the placement office at your alma mater or the state university nearest your preferred location. You might also contact placement offices at several other colleges or universities in your chosen area. In addition to these job listings, placement offices also register job applicants and submit resumes and resume summaries to companies seeking employees. The appropriate registration procedure will be discussed in Chapter 12 of this jobsearch manual. For the present, it is sufficient that you determine what publications are available to you and secure them for future use.

Foreign and American embassies and chambers of commerce. If you are interested in a job overseas with the subsidiary of an American company, if you are interested in working in America for the subsidiary of a foreign company, or if you are interested in working for a foreign company outside the United States, embassies are an excellent source of information. The French Embassy in Washington, D.C., for instance, publishes a list of all French subsidiaries in America showing the name, address, and principal business of both the parent and U.S. company. This and other such listings are available through the commercial attaché at no charge. The American Embassy and American Chamber of Commerce in foreign countries also publish such lists for U.S. subsidiaries overseas. American embassy addresses and the name of appropriate contacts can be obtained from the U.S. Printing Office directory, *Key Offices of Foreign Service Posts,* from your local federal information center, or from your congressional representative's office listed in the white pages of the telephone book. Foreign embassy addresses and telephone numbers in the United States can be obtained through telephone information in Washington, D.C., (202) 555-1212. Addresses for chambers of commerce overseas are available through your local chamber.

Special publications. The World Trade Academy Press, 50 East 42nd Street, New York, New York 10017, Telephone (212) 697-4999, publishes lists of American firms, subsidiaries, and affiliates operating in 85 different countries. Prices range from $6 to $9. They also publish lists of foreign firms operating in the United States for nine countries, as well as other special directories. They will send you prices and descriptions of these publications on request.

General Executive Services, Post Office Box 815, New Canaan, Connecticut 06840, Telephone (203) 966-1673, publishes a summary of classified help wanted advertisements on a weekly basis. This *Digest of Executive Opportunities* is available for the following specific areas of interest at approximately $95 each for a 20-week subscription:

Sales and Marketing	Finance/Data Software
Engineering/R&D	Administration
Manufacturing	International

Their source material includes 60 major newspapers, business publications, and trade magazines.

The American Management Associations, 135 West 50th Street, New York, New York 10020, Telephone (212) 586-8100, publishes an executive employment guide listing over 150 executive search or executive recruiting firms including several that offer a job registering service. This is available by mail for about $2 per copy. Executive search or recruiting firms are retained by companies to find and, in most cases, steal an individual with specific talent and experience from another firm. It is appropriate to advise such firms of your availability only if you are seeking a high-level position, will relocate, and have extensive experience specifically related to the job you seek. If this matches your search, order the list now. Its use is discussed in more detail in Chapter 12.

The Yellow Pages of your telephone directory. Substantial business information is available in this ubiquitous directory. It should not be neglected in your jobsearch campaign. Both your local library and your telephone company main office have out-of-state directories including Yellow Pages. In addition, they will usually be supplied to you free of charge by your local telephone company. Simply call the business office and explain that you plan to do telephone solicitation in conjunction with your jobsearch. They will send you the directories for your target cities, usually within a week or two. Although the information from this source does not include names of individuals or information concerning company size, it offers excellent listings of local companies by product categories. Frequently, additional information concerning officers' names and company size can be secured with a telephone call to the firm. *Who's Who in Finance and Industry* can also be a source for names of individuals in companies of interest to you.

SECRETARIAL SERVICES

Throughout your jobsearch campaign you will need competent secretarial services on a part-time basis. Most commercial secretarial services or temporary help companies are somewhat expensive and often inconvenient. As an alternative, you may have a friend or associate who is, or knows, a secretary who will work for you at night or do typing during his or her free periods. The current rate for such assistance is around $5 per hour. Most of our JOB-SEARCH clients found ready sources of secretarial assistance among friends who were lawyers and who, by the way, frequently had Mag-Card or other automatic typewriters. Other small business people — such as manufacturers' reps — are good possibilities.

The extent of this work in most campaigns will include primarily typing several resumes, answering approximately 10 to 20 help wanted ads per week, typing form letters and miscellaneous correspondence, and writing letters confirming each interview and telephone conversation regarding a job.

For all your typed work it is important that an electric business typewriter of high quality be used. It should have a carbon rather than a fabric ribbon. The type face should be standard typewriter characters. Do not use script, Roman, italics, or other unusual print.

The first impression you make on a prospective employer will frequently be in written form. At least in part, you will be judged by the appearance of this correspondence. It should be neat, attractive, and grammatically correct and should contain no spelling errors. Much of this will depend on the secretary you use. He or she should be chosen with care.

COPYING SERVICES

Three forms of copying or multiple reproduction will be required for your jobsearch campaign. Except for the direct mail letters, you will need copies of all correspondence. These can be either carbon copies or any legible, copying machine reproduction. For your resume, plain paper reproductions on a business copying machine, such as Xerox or IBM, will be needed. Automatic or magnetic card typing for multiple reproduction will be necessary for your direct mail marketing campaign.

Automatic typing equipment will individually type and address form letters on your letterhead at a rate in excess of one every two minutes. Companies offering such services are generally available in medium-size to large cities. They can be found under the listing for "Letter Shop Service" or "Advertising—Direct Mail" in the Yellow Pages of your telephone directory. Cost of these services should range from 40 to 60 cents per letter, depending on its length.

Call several of these firms to check rates. Also, find a convenient source of photocopying facilities. You may have a business friend or lawyer who can make his or her firm's equipment available to you.

FINANCIAL PLANNING

Do some financial planning prior to starting your major jobsearch effort. If you are employed, this might consist only of an estimate of the expenses involved in your search. More complete financial planning may be appropriate if you are unemployed. In this case, not only will you be required to pay for the search, but you must also support your family until you secure a new position.

It is wise to plan for a four-month jobsearch effort. Although the search can frequently be completed in a shorter period, it is preferable to eliminate a deadline controlled by economic considerations alone. A careful review of your expenses, financial strength, and potential sources of income will usually disclose that you can sustain your family without a regular salary for an extended period.

Forms (#10–#12) are included in this manual for calculating your net worth, estimating your monthly cash flow, and appraising your total jobsearch expense. Even though these may be only rough guesses, it is advisable for unemployed individuals to complete all three forms and for employed individuals to complete the jobsearch expense estimate. As situations change and new information is gained, the forms can be updated. This organization of finances will then allow you to plan your jobsearch more effectively and to devote more of your time and effort to this task.

CHAPTER 3

COMPILING AN ACCOMPLISHMENTS LIST

Of all the items of work involved in your jobsearch, the accomplishments list is one of the most important. You will use it throughout your campaign. It will form the basis for your resume and your direct mail sales letter. You will refer to it for other written correspondence and also immediately prior to going on job interviews. It should be prepared with care; it should be complete. When you are ready to work on it, reserve a morning or afternoon with three or four hours during which you can think and write without interruption.

As previously stated, you will not be hired by a new company because of your former titles or responsibilities. You will be hired to produce profits, or in the case of a nonprofit organization, to improve efficiency or provide services. The only real measure of your ability to contribute in these areas is your past accomplishments.

Use forms #13-#16 to list your career and other pertinent accomplishments. In all cases, each accomplishment should be described in one short phrase. Because these lists will be used as a reference for most of your correspondence, the phrases should be suitable for incorporation into your resume and letters. Make them direct and action oriented. Do not use superfluous words. The list should be complete. To the extent possible, include accomplishments that best relate to the job or jobs that are the objective of your campaign. Before you start to write, review some of the examples of resumes and letters in the appropriate sections of this manual. Note their phrasing and choice of words.

Wherever possible, quantify your accomplishments with numbers. Most persons, particularly business people, identify easily with numbers. They are concrete, are readily understood, and can be related to other sets of numbers. Instead of stating that you were responsible for a major increase in sales, say that you increased sales 30 percent, or by $200,000, in a one-year period. Instead of saying you substantially improved efficiencies, state that the improved efficiencies saved your company $30,000 yearly. Instead of stating that you managed the engineering department, indicate the total number of engineers under your direction, and the total dollar value of completed projects. Instead of stating that you have delivered talks to numerous professional groups, mention the total number of such groups and the number of participants.

In many cases the numbers you need will not be readily available. Leave blanks in your list and search out the information later. If the numbers cannot be found, put down your best guess — making every effort to be truthful. An estimate based on your best recollection is preferable to using a loosely defined word such as "large," "substantial," or "major." In fact, your accomplishments will serve you better if most qualifying words and adjectives are left out of your list entirely.

The majority of our JOBSEARCH clients complained that their accomplishments were difficult to describe — too general in nature or impossible to quantify. Yet they proceeded to assemble impressive lists of achievements. The only requirement is that you think about your past career as a series of objectives, tasks, and projects. JOBSEARCH's attorney clients found, for instance, that they could describe the number of cases they handled, the total monies at stake, and even the number of cases where they were able to avoid litigation — the bane of any business executive. Then they sold these desired skills and themselves. Look at Janet Parsons' resume (#25). She did an excellent job of turning a mundane position with a title insurance company into a challenging prospect as head of the right-of-way department with a major utility company.

In a few weeks you will be asking potential employers to pay you a salary to perform a job. Perhaps your requested salary will be higher than an employer wants to pay. This salary and the new position itself will depend on the return the employer expects to receive from the investment in you. Your past accomplishments will allow them to judge.

DIRECT JOB-RELATED ACCOMPLISHMENTS

The first three pages of your accomplishments list (#13) are to record all the accomplishments that are directly related to your past jobs and your responsibilities and performance in these jobs. Although all pertinent accomplishments should be recorded, each section should include several accomplishments that indicate a direct contribution to the profits or success of the company or organization. Do not neglect accomplishments of your subordinates performed under your direction or responsibility.

Never fall victim to the fear that you have no significant accomplishments. Ronald Marque had never worked directly in the field for which he was educated and wanted to enter (see his resume, #21). He spent hours reviewing his career, discussing it with his wife and colleagues. The result was a listed series of projects and studies that he could relate to financial analysis, some of which he had done during off hours with little apparent relation to the job he was hired to do. Now he is a senior financial analyst with a major shipbuilding company. An attractive peripheral aspect of this job is its proximity to water, permitting Ronald's indulgence in his favorite sport of sailing.

Your accomplishments should be listed by company in reverse chronological order. On the first line of each section show your title and the company name, city, and state. Under this, on the left, show the time period in years only, not months, such as 1971–1976. This should be done for each company. If you need additional pages, use lined tablet paper.

If you worked a long period of time with one company and acted in several different areas of responsibility or held several titles, separate these in the list as you would for different companies. Start a new section for each area of responsibility or title.

Think back over your career carefully. What was done better because you were there? What would not have been done had you not been there? What do you consider your most important or personally most satisfying direct job-related accomplishments?

INDIRECT JOB-RELATED ACCOMPLISHMENTS

On the fourth page of your accomplishments list (#14), record indirect job-related accomplishments. These are accomplishments performed as a result of a specific job but that were not directly related to the responsibilities of the job itself. If you were in sales, such an accomplishment might be teaching a sales training course for employees in another region of your company or outside it. Another example might be technical papers you wrote that were not required but were published for the benefit of your entire industry. A service performed for a professional or trade association in your industry would qualify as an indirect job-related accomplishment.

As with your direct job-related accomplishments, be specific and quantify wherever possible. If you conducted training classes, how many groups or individuals were involved? If you published a paper, to how many persons was it distributed?

EDUCATIONAL ACCOMPLISHMENTS

The next page of your list (#15) should show all the accomplishments related to your education that you felt to be most important or most satisfying. Do not include high school accomplishments unless you have only recently graduated or unless you attended a prominent preparatory or finishing school. The spaces provided are for college courses and activities, graduate work, and continuing education. On the first line of each section show the degree received or course completed, the name of the institution, the city, and the state. The space to the left is for the time period in years or the year the course was taken. Include both direct and indirect educational accomplishments; that is, list those relating directly to your studies and those, such as extracurricular activities, that you performed while attending school.

PERSONAL OR CIVIC ACCOMPLISHMENTS

The last page of the list (#16) is for those personal or civic accomplishments that you consider the most significant in your adult life. These might be accomplishments performed for civic or charitable organizations, for your church, or in line with your hobbies. In all instances, however, they should relate to or demonstrate your competence in some aspect of your work. If you are an engineer, for example, you might list assembling a color television kit. A major contribution to a fund-raising effort can demonstrate organizational or sales ability

After completing all four parts of your accomplishments list, wait a day and then go back and review all your accomplishments. Do they indicate a contribution to profits, efficiency, or the delivery of services? Do they show a willingness to work? Do they indicate awareness of what makes an organization successful? Most importantly, can they be used to sell you as an attractive investment for a new company?

CHAPTER 4

ESTABLISHING YOUR CAREER GOALS

Prior to setting the specific targets for your jobsearch campaign, you should establish or review your short- and long-term career goals. In your campaign you are not attempting just to find a job; you are trying to secure a career position. To do this it is necessary to target your efforts based on your career goals and, in the final stages of your search, to compare job opportunities with these short- and long-term objectives.

In reviewing hundreds of resumes and discussing careers, both past and future, with JOBSEARCH clients, we found that the most frequent mistake they made in career development was lack of planning. Too many men and women simply find a job with no thought of its impact on their future development. These persons later come to us, their resumes crowded with jobs of short duration. With each change of employment it becomes increasingly difficult to sell their past accomplishments and to locate the jobs they should have taken care to find years before. Don't let this happen to you.

Your career goals are composed of all the personal achievements and benefits that you expect from your job efforts. These goals should be specific, quantified, scheduled, and realistic. Instead of establishing "a top management position" as one of your goals, you should define this position perhaps as "vice-president of sales." Quantify the position by stating that it will be in a company grossing at least $10 million per year. Specify the time period within which you would like to attain this position. Then judge whether this objective is realistic in relation to your background, ambitions, and time frame.

Once you have established these goals, determine what sequence of events must occur, and what personal efforts or preparation you must undertake, to meet them. If, for instance, your ten-year objective is to be vice-president of sales and you are now a territory salesperson, you may identify it as desirable to be the top salesperson in your area. This would put you in a position to become an area sales manager. The subsequent steps might be district sales manager, regional manager, department head, and finally vice-president of sales. Do not neglect to identify additional training you might need, either in your job or through supplementary education.

Once established in written form, your career goals should be reviewed yearly. This review will determine whether your progress is consistent with your goals, as well as whether and how these goals should be modified. As you progress in your career, your objectives will and should change. You will continually gather data about yourself, your capabilities, and your job. You will also learn about your likes and dislikes, both in work and in private life. These and other such items will have an influence on your career objectives.

IMMEDIATE, FIVE-, AND TEN-YEAR OBJECTIVES

Use form #17 to record your career goals. When completing this form, note the following:

Position should include the title you wish as well as the area of responsibility, such as "vice-president—finance."

Salary should be stated in today's dollars, neglecting inflation.

Percent equity refers to your ownership in the company for which you work.

Scope of authority might be defined as your discretion in hiring and firing a specific number of employees, the extent of your control over the profit and loss of the organization, or the effect your decisions might have over the future course of the business.

Number of subordinates, direct refers to the number of employees reporting to you.

Number of subordinates, indirect refers to the total number of employees for whom you are responsible or who are beneath you on the company's organization chart.

Independence refers to the extent of your desire to work alone or work as a member of a team. It can be listed as strong, average, or weak.

Structured environment refers to your desire to work in an atmosphere of established procedures or one of a more flexible nature. It can be listed as highly, moderately, or loosely structured.

Recognition should indicate your desire in each of these categories as high, average, or unimportant to you regardless of whether the job might produce it.

PROCEDURE FOR DEFINING GOALS

If you cannot establish your career goals with assurance or are ambivalent about your vocation, examine yourself as well as your education, background, and work experience. This will assist you in formulating ideas. If you are young, do not be overly concerned that the available data are insufficient or incomplete. Use the data available and realize that your objectives will be affected by the experiences that lie before you in your career.

The following seven exercises will begin to give you ideas about yourself and your career. They can also help you choose a vocation or evaluate available vocational options.

1. Go back to your accomplishments lists and, for each accomplishment, indicate which you enjoyed, were ambivalent about, or disliked. You will find you accomplished more and enjoyed the work in areas where you have the greatest interest.
2. Make a list of your likes and dislikes. Include all you can think of in a general spectrum, and then star those that are work related.
3. Define yourself and your character by completing 20 sentences that respond to the question "Who am I?"
4. Make a list of everything that motivates you to work; then rank the items in the list 1, 2, 3, and so forth, highest motivating factor to lowest motivating factor.

5. For the perfect job, describe in short phrases its characteristics, the work involved, the relationships with people, its scope of authority, and its responsibilities.
6. For this perfect job, describe the changes that would make it still perfect in ten years' time.
7. List those jobs or tasks that your education and experience have trained you to do.

With the above information you can now go back to your career goals. Check each of these against your likes and dislikes, character, motivation, description of the perfect job, and training. If you find inconsistencies, determine what changes you need to make in your goals or in yourself.

If after completing the above work you would like to examine your vocation or investigate other vocations, an excellent source book is the *Dictionary of Occupational Titles* published by the U.S. Department of Labor. This two-volume set is available at most public libraries or may be purchased for about $20 from the Superintendent of Documents, U.S. Government Printing Office, Washington, D.C. 20402.

To use this dictionary, turn first to Appendix A of Volume Two, pages 649 and 650. This section gives an explanation of the three-digit code that relates each listed job to data, people, and things. Then review the "Worker Traits Arrangement of Titles and Codes" on pages 225 to 529 of Volume Two. This gives the work performed, worker requirements, and clues for relating applicants and requirements as well as the training and methods of entry for 176 career fields. It also gives classifications of jobs related to each field. Volume One of this dictionary lists over 35,000 job titles showing the work performed with a six-digit code relating to the worker traits discussed in Volume Two.

Although an examination of these books might at first appear to be a monumental task, they are arranged in a convenient format that can be skimmed to quickly determine the areas of interest to you. If these books serve no other purpose, they will give you a comprehensive view of the scope and opportunities available in the job market. They can be of assistance not only in reviewing your choice of vocation and your career goals, but also in establishing the specific target areas for your jobsearch marketing effort.

You may find the perfect job in the place you least expect. William G. Naff, #20 in the workbook section, was an accountant and controller. He is now the legal administrator for a 50-partner law firm, a job that includes not only accounting but control over every administrative aspect of a $7-million business. When he started his search he was unaware that such a position existed.

CHAPTER 5

TARGETING YOUR
MARKETING EFFORT

You are now ready to define the specific targets for your jobsearch marketing effort. For most campaigns at least three or four different targets should be pursued simultaneously. These might be similar to one another or may represent entirely different career options. All of them may be in the same industry or in different industries. They may be related to the same job responsibilities or entirely different responsibilities. The intent is to expand potential opportunities not only by covering a single market as thoroughly as possible but also by selling yourself into several different markets.

In many instances our clients used their jobsearch campaign as a method of choosing between different careers or career directions. They did this by establishing each career as a target and then evaluating the offers received in each.

One such case involved a young medical laboratory supervisor who came to us with the desire to break out of the confining environment of standard, automated medical testing. She wanted more contact with people and a greater opportunity for advancement. Although two of her targets related to the medical field outside the lab, her third was for personnel management. She wrote a separate resume and separate letters tying in her hiring and personnel work in the laboratory environment to this target. The job she finally chose was assistant personnel manager for one of the largest department store chains in her state, even though she had two other offers in health care.

When a person has substantial experience in one field and wishes to remain there, he or she may consider this only one target. Such a person should define second and third targets by considering a different type of organization, size of company, or geographical area even though these are all limited to his or her immediate background and expertise.

In these situations targets may be identical in all respects except one. This will be appropriate if that one difference is distinct enough to clearly define a separate set of options. For instance, your targets may differ only in geographical location. If you are limiting your primary search to one city, you may consider another even though it would not be quite as attractive. If you are conducting a nationwide search, perhaps you should also choose one city that appeals to you and concentrate a portion of your efforts there.

In defining your targets, do not neglect types of organizations outside your past experience. Many business skills are needed by associations and nonprofit groups of all types. Religious organizations need advertising skills. Fast-food franchisers need real estate lawyers. Large companies hire social counselors. Pulp and paper manufacturers hire lobbyists with environmental control experience. Trust departments of banks hire foresters. Improbable though it might seem, all these examples come from JOBSEARCH clients and the companies that now employ them. Use your imagination as they did. Do not arbitrarily limit your search.

In some jobsearch campaigns an individual may consider as many as five different targets. While this may occasionally be appropriate, it should be an exception for specific reasons. It is difficult to organize a massive effort with as many as five targets. This tends to make the search unwieldy. Different resumes and direct mail marketing letters will usually be required for each target. Different responses are required for each. Thus the effort can easily become dissipated to such an extent that it loses its effectiveness.

Within these constraints, the number and definition of targets is up to you. But they must all relate to your immediate and long-range objectives, as well as your past accomplishments. This should not limit your investigation of different careers, but for each target use your accomplishments to demonstrate your probable future success.

A word of caution, however. Don't try to sell yourself as a generalist. Throughout your business career, you have probably heard that companies want generalists. Although this may be true, they seldom hire them. Instead, they hire people with specific skills to do specific jobs. With the exception of entry-level positions, they expect these people to have gained enough experience to contribute in areas outside their specialized fields.

If you try to sell your general business skills, you will probably fail. Select your strongest skills or those readily salable. Select the specific areas in which you would like to work, and use these to establish your targets. But be specific.

If you have skills in several areas, fine. Use each to define a separate target. Do not fall into the trap of offering a potential employer a shopping list of jobs for which you are qualified. If you do this you probably won't be called even if a vacancy exists.

When you have completed defining your targets, go back and review your accomplishments list. Mark the accomplishments that relate best to each target area. Consider new, more appropriate wording or a different expression of the quantifying numbers for each target.

It is also advisable to relate your targets to the sources of information you investigated earlier. Go back to this list and review it to be certain the information you ordered is appropriate for the target areas chosen. If you can locate new sources of information, order them and add them to your list.

In establishing your targets, also take care that they are attractive to you. If you are considering a new industry, talk to a friend who is in that industry. From your information list, find another person in your local area and discuss with him or her the industry's environment and methods of operation. If you are considering a city away from your current home, it may be advisable to visit it and talk with real estate agents, bankers, and members of the chamber of commerce. This will also give you an opportunity to gather job information locally and purchase directories that will be needed for your search.

Be comfortable with your chosen targets. One of them may absorb 15 or more years of your working career.

ESTABLISHING TARGETS

Use form #18 to define the targets for your jobsearch marketing effort. When working on these target definitions, note the following:

Industries. Be as specific as possible. Instead of simply stating "manufacturing," state the products manufactured, the raw materials used, or the manufacturing processes involved—whichever is most appropriate to your jobsearch. If you have chosen a single industry for all target areas, it may be wise to go from the specific to the general. For instance, your first target might be the manufacture of plastic household utensils; your second target might be the manufacture of plastic articles for consumer or OEM (original equipment manufacturer) use; your third target might be manufacturing processes using extrusion or injection molding techniques.

Size of company, division, or organization. This should be stated in gross sales dollars per year or total number of employees, whichever relates more appropriately to the position you seek. In either case, indicate which is used and state the range that most accurately defines each target.

Type of company or organization. This should define the company as family-owned, publicly-owned, stock-exchange-listed, nonprofit, a professional partnership, a trade association, or other type of organization.

Geographical area. Again, be as specific as possible and, if appropriate, go from the specific to the more general. If you are limiting your search to your home city, unless the reasons are compelling, consider at least one target in a broader geographical area. An employer who wants you badly enough may offer an increase in salary that will more than compensate for the inconvenience of your moving. You cannot know this until you have found the opportunity and negotiated with the potential employer. This is particularly true for individuals at a high salary level. In an industrial city of one million people, there may be only 30 or 40 firms large enough to pay a vice-president of finance $40,000 a year. Adding three other large cities may increase the number of potential employers to over 200.

Position and responsibilities. This should include your desired title and a short description of the responsibilities you expect to exercise. If possible, define these responsibilities by such items as the number of employees under your supervision, the territory for which you might be responsible, or the total sales or manufacturing cost over which you might have control.

Personal preference. Review the targets you have defined and rank them first, second, and third, according to your personal preference.

Career preferences. As above, rank your targets according to their probable effect on your career goals.

CHAPTER 6

PREPARING YOUR RESUME

Much has been written about resumes — their preparation, style, layout, wording, and content. While all these items are important in a resume, they are no more important than in any other written business communication. In addition, most of the published material concerning resumes assumes that this document will have widespread use in any job campaign and will be an important factor in its success or failure. In your own jobsearch campaign this will not be the case. You will make limited use of the resume.

HOW EMPLOYERS USE RESUMES

In 1971, when I was president of a small brick-manufacturing firm, I ran a three-line help wanted classified advertisement requesting a plant manager at $15,000 per year. It was placed for one day only in the Eastern Edition of *The Wall Street Journal*. It attracted 200 replies. A larger display ad in this paper can easily draw more than 1,000 replies, while local classified display ads frequently produce 500 or more responses. Most of these are in the form of resumes, both with and without cover letters.

The result is that some member of or team of individuals from the company or agency must read these resumes. They have no choice but to organize the task into a manageable format. This can be done only by skimming each resume, giving it 30 to 45 seconds.

The reader usually establishes a set of somewhat arbitrary criteria to use in this skimming process. Because judging a candidate's job qualifications is a difficult task, the criteria selected will have little to do with the candidate's ability to perform in the desired position. Instead, for instance, the reviewer will decide not to consider anyone under 30, over 40, without a college degree, having more than two jobs in ten years, or lacking experience in the reviewer's industry.

The reader picks up each resume and consciously or unconsciously thinks, "What in this document automatically allows me to eliminate this candidate?" This is done with no disdain for the candidates. It is simply a convenient method to reduce the total responses to a manageable number. Spending 45 seconds on each of 200 resumes will require over two and a half hours reading time. If more time than this is spent on each resume, the first will have been forgotten long before the last is read.

Thus reduced to 20 or 30 candidates, the reviewer will then read the entire resume—if it is no more than two pages long. Reading two typewritten pages takes two and a half to five minutes. At best, this is still an hour and a half to two hours of reading. Again the emphasis is on elimination. The purpose is to reduce the number of candidates to four or five. These the company will take the time and expense to interview personally. Once this is done the resume has served its purpose. It has been used to eliminate over 95 percent of the candidates who responded to the company's advertisement.

In most companies of medium to large size, all the above described work will be done by one or more members of the personnel department. Because their primary function in the hiring process is to screen—that is, eliminate—applicants, they want resumes with maximum information included. These members of the personnel department, however, do not have the authority to hire new employees.

No manager of a department will allow some other person in the company to hire people who will work for him or her. Instead, the personnel department will be requested to present the manager with three or four of the best candidates. These persons will subsequently be interviewed by the department head, who will then hire the candidate he or she wants. While it is difficult to avoid personnel departments entirely, it is important to be cognizant of their function and to realize why they invariably request resumes. Members of personnel should be avoided tactfully whenever possible.

It is also important that you remember the use of the resume in the job-seeking process. Almost invariably it is a negative instrument. In your own jobsearch campaign you will limit its distribution to those areas and occasions where it can become positive.

You need a resume. It should be a good one, but its use must be closely controlled.

HOW YOU SHOULD USE A RESUME

In your jobsearch campaign the most appropriate use of the resume is as a means of communication between someone who knows or has met you and another interested party. If, for instance, you have been interviewed by a member of a company, you should follow up by giving that person your resume. Then, in talking with other people in the company, he or she can give them a copy of the resume, along with impressions of you and an expression of interest in your background, experience, and abilities. As the reader then searches for the areas of interest spotlighted by his or her colleague, the resume will become a positive instrument.

In the early stages of your campaign, your resume will be given only to individuals and organizations that might pass it on to potential employers. In almost all such instances, this will be done with a covering letter or verbal explanation showing some interest in you.

It will be appropriate for you to send a copy of your resume to—or leave it with—all personal contacts you use in your campaign. Also, give your resume to other persons or firms who do not represent potential employers but who may know of organizations that might be interested in you. These will include employment agencies or executive recruiters, as well as college placement officers and some trade associations.

In the job market, these individuals and organizations are interested in offering assistance to both employer and employee. In the case of employment agencies and executive recruiters, a commission for this assistance is expected. Although not always the case, particularly with employment agencies, most of these individuals and organizations will transmit your resume to interested firms with some indication of your ability to contribute to their company.

Do not use your resume in answering help wanted advertisements or in your mail marketing campaign. Even if a help wanted advertisement requests that a resume be sent, do not send one. When answering these advertisements, there is no reason to give a potential employer sufficient information to eliminate you for reasons unrelated to your qualifications for the job. Instead you will give only enough information to interest the employer in talking with you personally. For similar reasons you will not send a cover letter and resume in your mail marketing campaign. You will choose the alternative of a well-executed sales letter designed to arouse the interest of the reader.

One of our JOBSEARCH clients, for example, answered an ad in a large regional newspaper for a public relations director at $32,000 per year. Although the ad requested a resume, he sent only a letter. Of the 264 respondents, he was one of the six who were called. He got the job. Had he replied by sending his resume, however, he would not even have had an interview. The ad specifically requested five years of experience; he had only four. Although this would have shown in his resume, he did not have to mention it in a letter. He had only to describe his substantial accomplishments in the public relations field.

In the latter stages of your jobsearch campaign, you will use your resume to confirm and support your discussions in personal interviews. In these cases your resume will be given or sent to the interviewer at the end, rather than the beginning, of the interview.

Each of the above uses of your resume will be discussed in more detail in the appropriate section of this manual. In most jobsearch campaigns, 25 to 50 copies of the resume will be sufficient. The only exceptions to this might be a broad canvassing of executive recruiting firms or a large number of personal contacts for a national campaign where 100 to 150 additional copies will be required.

LAYOUT

There are five basic approaches to resume preparation. These are:

1. *Chronological*—work experience arranged in reverse chronological order by employer.
2. *Functional*—work experience arranged according to function or responsibilities exercised with little regard to chronological order or different employers.
3. *Organizational*—work experience listed according to companies or organizations, frequently without regard to chronological order.
4. *Narrative*—work experience written in a continuous narrative style.
5. *Creative*—entire resume in its layout, wording and use of artistic or other embellishments considered as creative in style.

Although each of these formats has an appropriate use in some campaigns, in this jobsearch manual only the chronological and functional style of resume will be considered. The narrative resume is difficult and time consuming to read. The creative resume too frequently becomes a gimmick that works to the disadvantage of the job candidate. The organizational resume is a modified chronological form that in most cases is better presented in its more acceptable style.

The chronological and functional resumes are by far the most common and are generally more acceptable to the recipient. In addition, the resume will be used in your jobsearch campaign more as a sales tool than as a complete recitation of your career history. It can therefore be a straightforward presentation of your accomplishments and experience that enhances your case for employment.

In most jobsearch campaigns the chronological form of resume will be preferred. It is easy to read and understand. It also presents the work experience of the job candidate in the expected order of importance to the reader. The potential employer is more interested in your accomplishments last year than in those of ten years ago. This is particularly true when your recent accomplishments have a more direct relation to the job you seek than those of your earlier career. Most job seekers, attempting to take maximum advantage of career progression in their new position, will find this to be the case.

When your most recent experiences do not relate to the position you seek, the functional style of resume should be considered. This style can be used effectively by those who have held a large number of jobs of short duration. It can also be used by persons who have had a long career that included responsibilities over several different areas with only one or two employers. In these instances the work experience, grouped according to function, can be arranged in the order of maximum advantage to the job seeker. Several jobs with different companies can, for instance, be grouped in one functional paragraph.

In the functional resume it is appropriate, unless reasons are compelling to the contrary, to indicate the total duration in years — not necessarily including dates — for each function exercised. The jobsearch resume form for your first rough draft (#19) is set out in a chronological format. To change this to a functional format, simply list your title or functional responsibilities in the space provided for the company name, and include the time period in the text rather than in the left-hand column. In some cases names of companies worked for and dates of employment are included, one line for each, at the end of the professional history section. Except for these changes, the layout for functional and chronological resumes is identical.

The resume layout preferred in this manual places all headings in the left-hand column. All biographical data are given first, followed by professional highlights, professional history, special items of interest, and references, in that order. The intent is to make the job candidate appear first as a human being rather than as mere words on a page. The initial biographical section will contain items to which the reader can readily relate. Children, for instance, hold a special position in most families, and the reader might remember when his or her children were the ages that yours are. The reader may also relate to your age, may have known people from your home town, or may otherwise start to visualize you as a person as he or she reads this section.

Next comes "Professional Highlights." This is a summary of your career accomplishments that are most pertinent to the job you seek. With his or her interest thus stimulated, the reader will review your professional history with more attention than he or she might otherwise have given it.

In considering the layout of your resume, it is imperative that it be neat, well organized, and balanced on the page. It should be no more than two pages long. You may find it necessary to retype it several times in order to adjust the margins or the spacing. This should be done until you feel it is correct in every respect. Examples of both chronological and functional resumes can be found in the jobsearch workbook (#20–#25).

PHOTOGRAPH

The layout of the biographical data in the jobsearch resume form provides a space for your photograph in the upper right-hand corner. Generally it is most convenient to staple the photograph to the page. As an alternative you might use the new, stick-type glues available at most stationery stores. Do not have your photograph printed as part of the resume.

Because of the expense involved, resumes with your photograph should be used only for the most important contacts in your jobsearch campaign — for example, after an interview for a job of particular interest to you, or with a personal contact who has a specific job vacancy or company in mind that fits your objectives.

The extent of their use will depend, more than anything else, on your financial situation. If they can be secured inexpensively, you may wish to put the photograph on all resumes distributed. They enhance your presentation.

COPYING

Your resume should be reproduced on a good-quality, plain-paper copying machine such as Xerox or IBM. Most coated-paper and other wet-process copiers do not provide as neat and true an image as dry-process, plain-paper copiers. In addition, the coated-paper stock is not at all similar to your stationery and will not offer as attractive a package when mailed with a cover letter. Use white bond paper. The use of colored paper is a gimmick to be avoided.

In no case should your resume be offset printed or otherwise produced in a printed, commercial form. Most processes of this type are used when a hundred or more copies are required. Your intent is to make the reader feel that he or she is one of only a few recipients of the resume, not one of several hundred to whom it has been distributed en masse.

DRAFT AND WORDING

Follow the jobsearch resume form (#19). Prior to beginning work on your first draft, review the job targets you established for your marketing effort. Then decide how many different resumes you intend to write. The possibilities to consider are these:

> A single resume for the entire jobsearch campaign where your marketing targets are similar in position and responsibilities.

> Different "Professional Highlights" sections for different targets with all other aspects of the resume identical.

> A functional-style resume with a different arrangement of the functions under "Professional History" and a different "Professional Highlights" section for each target.

> Separate resumes for each target with substantial differences in wording and, perhaps, in style.

In making these decisions, be certain of the appropriateness of your resume for each job you seek.

When you are ready to start, pick your first-priority target and complete the resume form for that target. You can then work on drafts for your other resumes using this first one as a guide.

For the first draft, do the biographical section first, from "Name" through "Education." Then complete the "Professional History" section including "Professional Organizations," "Military Service," and "Special Items of Interest." After these have been written, complete the "Professional Highlights" section. "References" should be added after you have checked their responses as discussed in Chapter 7.

Use no abbreviations in your resume. Spell out the names of all states, universities, and organizations. Take particular care that any trade or professional jargon you use is suitable to the position you seek. Unless it contributes to a demonstration of your competence, limit the use of such language or avoid it completely. Do not use the word "I." Write your sentences as if its inclusion were implied.

Use a direct and active writing style. Keep your sentences short and to the point. Instead of saying "was responsible for supervision of the entire sales force," simply put "supervised the entire 50-person sales force." Instead of saying "cost control procedures were revised," use the shorter and more active "revised cost control procedures."

Finally, and extremely important, the spelling, punctuation, and grammar must be correct.

For each resume, exercise your own judgment in deciding which sections should be emphasized. For instance, if your military service was short, it should be placed after the "Professional History" section as shown. If, however, it was a significant portion of your career experience, it should be included under "Professional History" with other positions held. If you are weak in education but strong in experience, relocate the "Education" section immediately after "Military Service."

Your entire resume should be accomplishments oriented. Prior to beginning work on your resume, review your accomplishments list in detail. For the "Professional Highlights" section, pick the three or four most outstanding accomplishments of your career that relate to the job you seek. For "Professional History," review your accomplishments list again and include the most pertinent accomplishments for each company or function without repeating those used in the "Highlights" section. If you must repeat, change the wording or expression of the quantifying statistics. Under "Professional History," for instance, you might say, "cut overhead costs by $100,000 per year." In the "Highlights" section this could read, "reduced overhead 24% annually."

Where you show a title held or describe responsibilities exercised, also include the result. Instead of saying you were an area salesperson responsible for industrial clients in North Alabama, go on to say that you increased sales 30 percent during this period. If you were a plant manager responsible for production costs, include the amount these costs decreased during your tenure or the fact that they increased only 10 percent while material and labor costs increased 16 percent. Among your accomplishments, find measures of your performance that indicate your contribution to the success or profit of the organization and include them.

When writing your resume, be honest with yourself and your future employer. Your objective, however, is to cast your career in the best light possible. Do this unabashedly; be boastful. It is your career. They are your accomplishments. List them in a manner that will facilitate the reader's evaluation of your probable contribution to his or her organization and will also enhance your candidacy. The employer must decide whether to make a sizable investment in you. Your intent is to influence this decision to the maximum extent possible.

Let your accomplishments speak for themselves, however. Minimize the use of self-laudatory words such as "greatest," "best," and "outstanding." Eliminate meaningless, supercilious adjectives such as "largest," "major," and "substantial." Do not use the word "very" in this or any other written correspondence. Because of its overuse it now tends to have the opposite effect to that desired.

Six sample resumes, four of the chronological and two of the functional style, are given in the workbook, #20–#25. Review these with care. Pay particular attention to the style, language, and order of presentation for each.

When completing your first resume draft, note the following:

1. The words "Personal Resume" should be typed near the top of the page with the month and year immediately underneath. Both typed lines should be centered. Use the month when you will most likely give your first resume to a job contact.

2. *Name.* Show your last name first, written in capital letters. Given names should be written in upper and lower case. No nicknames should be used. If you are usually called by a nickname, this can best be mentioned in a personal interview. If your last name is particularly difficult to pronounce, you may wish to include a phonetic spelling of it in parentheses on the line below it.

3. *Address.* Show your house number and street on one line. Give city, state, and zip code on another. Your residential address only should be shown.

4. *Telephone.* Show your area code and home number. If you can receive calls concerning employment at work, give your office telephone number and indicate which is which. Include your area code even if your search is limited to your local area.

5. Under *Civil Status,* include birth date, city and state of birth, citizenship if pertinent, and marital or single status. Write these facts in brief narrative style as shown in the examples.

6. Include information concerning your wife (or husband), if you think it is pertinent. Your wife's maiden name may be

included if she or her family is well known in the area where you seek employment. Her citizenship may be included if it is not the same as yours or is pertinent to a foreign position you seek.

7. In general, do not indicate that you are divorced unless you feel that being single at your age might raise more questions than a divorce.

8. *Children.* List numbers of daughters and sons, showing ages. Do not include names of your children. It is not necessary to indicate that older children are no longer living with you. This will be inferred and is of little importance. If your children have graduated from college, you might include this information because it reflects on you.

9. *Languages.* Include only those foreign languages with which you are fairly conversant. Indicate your fluency in speaking, reading, or writing. If you imply proficiency, be careful that you can demonstrate it. You may be surprised to find that your interviewer is also proficient in that language and will use it in a part of the interview.

10. *Education.* List degrees attained in reverse chronological order starting with graduate school, then university or college. Include high school information only if it is an outstanding school that might be known to the reader or if you received some honor that might be pertinent to your job campaign. Under "Graduate" or "University," include a complete description of the degree you received. Mention minor subjects only if they are pertinent to the job you seek. Include any honors you received. Under "Continuing Education," list night courses or special education courses taken during your career. If this list is long, include only those courses that were business related.

11. *Professional Highlights.* Write this section last. It should be a short one-paragraph summary of your recent job history and most important accomplishments. Do not list company names, but include recent titles and responsibilities, followed by accomplishments that demonstrate a contribution to profits, cost reductions, increases in sales, production efficiencies, or the success of the organization. Those accomplishments that can be quantified with numbers are most important in this section. Indications of the scope of these accomplishments and their impact on the company are also

important. A potential employer skimming your resume may read only this far. These highlights should make the reader want to read further. Write and rewrite this section; refer to your accomplishments list; refer to your job history. Make this paragraph relevant to the job you are seeking. It is the most important paragraph in your resume.

12. *Professional History.* For the chronological style of resume, your career history should be listed in reverse chronological order. The first line should include the name of the company and the city and state where you worked. The company name should be underlined. If it was a large company, include the name of the division or subsidiary. On the second line, show the dates of your employment in years only, not months. The months are unimportant in the reader's eyes. In addition, showing only the years will eliminate obvious periods of unemployment that might otherwise require explanation.

For each company or major job responsibility, write a short paragraph. The first sentence should include your most recent title and a statement of the size and type of organization, including—for a manufacturing company— the major products produced. The second sentence can include a short description of the responsibilities exercised, ending with a result or accomplishment. The following sentences should include several other accomplishments. If you held more than one position and worked for this company for a considerable period, you may wish to include the appropriate years in the left-hand column adjacent to the beginning sentence defining that position.

Proceed in similar fashion throughout your history, listing each company for which you worked. As you go further back in time your paragraphs and descriptions should become shorter. For jobs you held in the distant past, at the beginning of your career, you may wish to include only the company and responsibilities with appropriate dates.

13. *Military Service.* Show branch, rank achieved, period in service by years, and any specific assignments, duties, or accomplishments that can be related to private business.

14. *Professional Organizations.* List only organizations, and any official positions held, that relate to your business career.

15. *Special Items of Interest.* List items of specific interest not covered above—such as articles you have published, special

honors you have received, business licenses or patents you hold, speeches you have made to professional or business organizations, and your outside activities or hobbies — only if they relate to your business career or the employment you seek.

16. *References.* For this portion of your resume, refer to Chapter 7 of this jobsearch manual.

ITEMS TO AVOID

In most cases your resume should not include information or items other than those discussed above. The only exceptions would be items directly related to your career history, your accomplishments, or the position you are seeking. Social work performed during several years might be an example.

As already pointed out, the resume as it is commonly used is a negative instrument. For this reason, you should not include any information that could be construed as a negative reference to your career or personality. These items can best be explained in a personal interview.

Other items to avoid are these:

Salary. Do not include any mention of past salaries or desired salary. A resume is not the place to indicate the salary you might expect in your new position. This is a point of negotiation that should be brought up only after a potential employer has decided to hire you for a job. In addition, you may be considered for a job with compensation that far exceeds your highest career salary. You do not want to be eliminated by showing that previous salaries have not been in this range.

Reasons for changes in employment. Explanation of such changes is frequently awkward and should not be attempted in a resume. The reasons for a change in employment may have been personal, or you may have been fired. Regardless, they have little to do with your accomplishments. The subject should be deferred for a full discussion in a job interview and, even then, only if you are questioned on the point.

Desired position. Discussions of your job objectives, availability, desired location, or willingness to travel should not be included in your resume. They should be part of a letter or subsequent job interview. In particular, all mention of job objectives should be avoided. Nothing will dampen the impact of your resume more than some arrogant reference to your wanting a job "in a responsible management position that will allow me to realize my full potential while contributing to the success of the company."

Other items. Do not include any of the following miscellaneous, unrelated bits of information: height and weight, health status, race, sex, supervisors' names and titles, unrelated hobbies, sports interests, test scores, academic grades other than top class standing, church affiliation, family background, home ownership, Social Security number, or driver's license number. If a company wants to hire you, do you really think it will care whether you are 5 feet 5 inches or 6 feet 3 inches tall? Leave this information for employment application forms.

HANDLING PROBLEMS

Because your resume will have limited use in your jobsearch campaign, it is not difficult to handle special problems such as age, lack of experience, overly specialized experience, frequent job changes, and career changes. Notwithstanding, you should direct some care and attention to these areas.

If you are advanced in age, your resume should emphasize experience and, wherever possible, a long list of accomplishments and progression in your career. These should be directed toward one or two specific areas in which you can make an immediate contribution. You might find an employer with special problems who would welcome having a 60-year-old man with 30 years of experience to solve problems within the five- to ten-year period before his retirement.

If you lack experience in the field you wish to enter, emphasize accomplishments indicating that your intelligence and drive will more than compensate for the problems associated with a career change. Any similar changes in positions or responsibilities in your past career should be emphasized along with accomplishments that show the change was successful.

If you have highly specialized experience in a field that is not your current target, describe your accomplishments in terms that show their application or impact in a broader area. Mention work or participation in company decisions outside your specialty. Drop all jargon used in your field and substitute general business terms.

This is particularly important when you are making a change from the military, government, or education field to private industry. Most business executives have a bias against such persons because of their presumed lack of experience with profit incentives. You can best overcome this in your resume by stressing accomplishments that relate to cost reductions or demonstrate a concern for costs and efficiency. In addition, the use of business terms and expressions is particularly important. Review your accomplishments and ask yourself if they would read the same if your employer had been a business organization.

If you have changed jobs frequently or held jobs of short duration, it may be wise to omit all reference to some of them. These may be considered as temporary or exploratory positions that did not work out. As such, they do not have to be included as part of your career history.

Your resume is a sales tool and should be treated as such. Write it in positive terms. Keep it accomplishments oriented, and consider carefully how problems should be phrased in relation to your specific job targets.

CHAPTER 7

REFERENCES

Your choice of references can be critical to your jobsearch campaign. At some stage in considering you as a potential employee, virtually all companies will phone your references. They will want to discuss your work habits, personality traits, and past performance. Because these responses are important to the potential employer, it is not enough that you choose your references with care. Their responses must also be checked, and you must maintain close contact with them throughout your campaign.

Never include a line in your resume stating, "References available upon request." If they are available, they should be listed. Do not force a potentially interested employer to request these names. You have nothing to hide and can expect your references to make a strong, positive statement about you. Because of the limited use made of the resume in your jobsearch, there is little likelihood that your references will be inconvenienced by too many phone calls.

Once chosen, list your references at the end of your resume. This should include the full name, title, company affiliation, city and state of residence, and telephone number. Because reference checks are usually made by telephone, it is not necessary to show full addresses.

References should not be listed in the order of best or worst. It can be damaging if the response becomes less favorable as more references are called. This might suggest to the caller that additional references would continue in this pattern. For this reason you may consider listing your best reference second.

Three references should be chosen. This is a convenient number to call and, with similar response from each, should be sufficient. If more are needed by any particular company, they will be requested.

CHOICE OF REFERENCES

All three of your references should be business people who have known you well in one or more of your recent jobs. If possible, these should be jobs that relate closely to the position you seek. It is always advisable to include a reference from your last employer if it is a good one. If this cannot be done, be ready to explain why. An interested company may specifically ask to talk with your last supervisor. When you have substantially different job targets and resumes, you might consider listing different references or listing the references in a different order for each.

Your references should be persons in an equal or superior position to the one for which you are applying. It is advisable to have one reference whose position is above or similar to that of the probable caller. The only exception to these rules might be a reference who reported to you or worked under you in a former job. This might be appropriate if a major aspect of your new job would be supervision over similar employees. This exception, however, must be handled with care. In the eyes of many business people, a subordinate is not always the best judge of his or her immediate superior. In addition, subordinates do not generally enjoy as close a business and social relationship with their superiors as people who are of equal or higher rank do.

Do not use personal references such as your minister, neighbors, or close friends who have had no contact with you in business. Any prospective employers checking your references will expect your business associates to be as conversant with your honesty and personality traits as your friends. In addition, they are most interested in these traits as they appear in a business environment. Your references should be persons who know you well in both a business and a social context wherever possible.

CHECKING REFERENCE RESPONSES

You cannot choose your references on the basis of what you think they will say about you. You must know what they will say and how they will say it.

Too often our JOBSEARCH clients gave us references they considered excellent—old friends who would surely want to help. On calling them for the check, we found that they did indeed want to help, but they occasionally made a seemingly innocuous statement that would have destroyed the interest of any prospective employer.

Otherwise excellent references may volunteer too much information about you, your personal life, or your negative traits no matter how slight. Others might mention health problems that were brought under control years before. You cannot afford to leave these responses to chance.

Although checking a reference's response is not difficult, it must be done with care. It can be harmful if the reference finds you are privy to information he or she considered confidential.

Ideally, your references should be checked by a close business associate or friend whom they do not know. You should meet with this friend or associate and explain in detail the objectives of your search and your approach to the job market. He or she should understand that your reference check is not the result of any curiosity or anxiety on your part but only one aspect of a well-planned, well-executed job campaign. The person checking your references should be given a copy of your draft resume—typed, if possible—and a description of your job targets. Immediately before phoning each reference, he or she should read this information and be familiar with its contents.

Give your friend or associate four or five references to be called, and explain that you intend to use the best three. Also give your intermediary copies of the list of questions to be asked; request that the answers be written down. After each call, notes should be made concerning its general aspects and tone.

A suggested list of questions for a reference check (#26) is set out in a form that can be copied and filled in for each call. ("He" and "him," of course, become "she" and "her" if the candidate is a woman.) Because this list is general and too long for most calls, you or the person performing the reference check should edit it before or during each telephone conversation. Eliminate irrelevant questions and add questions that relate directly to your past or the position you seek.

The person performing this check should telephone each reference, introduce himself or herself using a real or a fictitious name, and state that the call is being made because you listed the other party as a reference on your resume. The caller can then request a few minutes to ask questions about you. The reference should be given the impression or told directly that the caller is interested in hiring you. Another option we sometimes used at JOBSEARCH was to have the caller describe himself or herself as an executive recruiter. This stratagem precludes possibly embarrassing questions about the fictitious company that the caller may not be able to answer.

Do not be present while the reference check calls are made, but meet with the caller at the earliest mutual convenience after they have been completed. You and the person performing the check can then review responses, including not only answers to the questions but also the general impression the reference made on the caller. If you do not find three acceptable references from these initial calls, continue the procedure until you have three in whose response you have unquestionable faith.

In making decisions concerning your references, consider that some slightly negative information about you is desirable. It is for this reason that the person performing your reference check should specifically ask about any negative characteristics or traits you might have. This negative information will lend credence to the preponderance of positive statements about you and your career. This is particularly advantageous if the negative information or trait would in some cases be viewed as a benefit. For instance, a reference might state that you are sometimes overly aggressive or that you demand too much of your subordinates or yourself.

The best reference is not a sugarcoated recital of the traits of the perfect worker. Your reference should know you well enough to speak of your weaknesses as well as your strengths. These, however, should not be weaknesses that would have a negative impact on your suitability for the job.

COMMUNICATING WITH YOUR REFERENCES

After your references have been chosen and their responses checked, contact each of them and then keep them advised of your progress. Your initial contact should be made just prior to giving out your first resumes, as late as possible in the campaign. In this way your conversation with your references will be near the time they might receive calls.

Try to meet with each of your references personally. If this is not possible, phone them. In this first conversation, request permission to use them as a reference. The reference may mention that he or she has already been called. You can explain that you were pursuing an initial job possibility but that you have now expanded your search to include a much wider range of potential opportunities.

Ask the reference to accentuate the positive and even help directly in your career change or advancement, but also request that the statements be both frank and honest. Explain your approach to the job market, as well as the targets and objectives you have established. Tell your reference that you will send him or her a copy of your resume as soon as it is completed.

Do not take a copy of the resume to this first meeting. It would be presumptuous to give your reference a resume with his or her name already on it, before permission has been requested to include it.

Following this initial contact, write a letter to each of your references and enclose a copy of your completed, typed resume. This letter should express gratitude for assistance given to your campaign, and should summarize again the objectives of your search. Tell each reference that you will keep him or her advised of your progress. (See #27 for a letter of this type.)

Then, as you proceed through your campaign, phone each reference periodically to report on your progress. This will also give you an opportunity to learn the names of the companies that have called and to again thank your references for their assistance. You might also phone them after any particularly interesting job interview, discuss the position with them, and forewarn them of possible calls.

At the successful conclusion of your jobsearch campaign, advise your references of the new position you have accepted and thank them for the contribution they made to the success of your effort. They will appreciate this recognition. In addition, you may wish to call on them again for assistance as you work toward your career goals.

PART TWO

MARKETING

CHAPTER 8

MARKETING YOURSELF

You have now completed all the preliminary work, established your information sources, and prepared the basic written materials you will need to execute your jobsearch campaign. You are ready to begin making initial contacts with the job market. In this phase of the program five methods will be used to introduce you to potential employers. These are personal contacts, answering help wanted advertisements, a direct mail campaign, other contacts, and developing special situations.

Emphasis placed on each of these will depend on individual circumstances. With the possible exception of developing special situations, virtually all job seekers will make at least some use of each.

Throughout this phase of your program the objective is to secure the maximum number of personal interviews with potentially interested employers. Maximize these opportunities by being expansive. If you are in doubt about a contact, make it. If you are attracted by a help wanted advertisement but feel your qualifications might not be adequate, answer it. If a little more work is required to expand your mailing list, do it.

Make as many contacts with the market as the information and time available to you permit. This jobsearch manual shows you how to make and organize these contacts with a minimum of effort. In most campaigns you should be able to make your talent and experience known to between 200 and 500 individuals and organizations.

Because these will result in a number of personal meetings and interviews, it will be convenient to have a standard business appointments diary. These are available at most office supply outlets. As you set up appointments, enter them in the diary. You may also wish to block out certain periods during each day to devote to other aspects of your jobsearch campaign.

CONFIRMING LETTERS

This jobsearch manual stresses one cardinal rule. Do not contact anyone concerning a job either by telephone or in a meeting without confirming this contact in a letter. This refers to all persons who are in a position to help you or who represent a potentially interested employer. Examples of such confirming letters and an explanation of their content are included at each appropriate point in the following chapters of this manual.

These letters are not only polite, they are often a pleasant, unexpected reminder to the recipient that you appreciate the assistance or consideration being given. They remind the recipient of the expected follow-up to your conversations and do not allow him or her to forget you and the objectives of your search.

In the business world, letters of this type are so rare they will do more to advance your job campaign than any other single item. I have talked to directors of personnel who have interviewed thousands of job candidates. They tell me that less than one percent confirm their interviews in writing. Consequently, these few individuals are recognized for their thoughtfulness and effort and immediately have an edge over other candidates.

One JOBSEARCH client went on a full day's interview at a company's corporate headquarters in the State of Washington. He met individually with nine officers during the day. After returning home he wrote each man and woman he had met. The letters were short, and the wording of each was varied to avoid embarrassment if the recipients compared notes. He got the job over two other finalists who had the same opportunity.

CHAPTER 9

PERSONAL CONTACTS

Personal contacts are defined as those individuals in business who are in a position to help you and would want to help. They might be close friends, customers, or former associates. Because your initial contacts with these people should be made by telephone and, wherever possible, in a personal meeting, they should be limited in most jobsearch campaigns to approximately 20 individuals. More than this number will become cumbersome and too time consuming.

An exception to this might be a campaign conducted by a well-known executive in a national firm. He may wish to solicit help from 40 to 50 business associates spread over the entire United States. This can be handled best as a part of his direct mail campaign by writing a letter similar to that used for executive recruiters. He could then add a personal note at the end of each letter and enclose his resume just as would be done with other personal contacts.

In some instances you may know of only two or three individuals who will be in a position to assist you in your jobsearch campaign. Even with so short a list, you should not neglect these people. They may suggest a company or send your resume to a friend who needs you.

Because your personal contacts do not usually represent potential employers, they may put you in touch with other interested parties and should be consulted early in your campaign. Job interviews from these sources, therefore, will more closely correspond to interviews secured later through more direct methods.

WHOM TO CONTACT

Use a number of sources to compile your personal contacts list. Search your memory. If they're available, review your old business files and correspondence. Look over your Christmas card mailing list. If you were married less than five years ago and had a well-attended ceremony, review the invitation list to your wedding. Talk to members of your family and close business associates.

List everyone who would be interested in helping you. Do not waste your time contacting people who might want to help but who are not in a position to know of potential employers that match your job targets. Your best contacts will be executives directly related to the business in which you hope to be employed. This includes customers, suppliers, or participants in this industry. The next more preferable contacts would be business executives indirectly related to the industry of your choice. This includes members of banks, law firms, accounting firms, advertising agencies, or business consulting firms that have contacts with or knowledge of this industry. Finally, your contacts may include persons who are not related to the industry of your choice but who might be able to suggest your candidacy to other business people. This might include executives of civic organizations who are well known in their community or have an outstanding reputation in the business world.

All of these personal contacts should be entered on list #28, giving the name, title, company affiliation, business address, and telephone number of each. Space is provided to record the required follow-up as well as any subsequent contacts generated for you by these individuals. The list should be kept in the "Personal Contacts" section of your notebook, followed by copies of all correspondence with these individuals.

Make as many copies of the form as will be needed for your total number of contacts. Space is provided for five on each page.

HOW TO CONTACT

After you have completed your list, establish a schedule for making these contacts. Phone all individuals in your local area and request an appointment to meet with them personally. If you feel it is appropriate, tell them you are starting a jobsearch campaign and would like to discuss it with them. At these meetings, review your approach to the job market and describe your objectives and job targets. Ask for their comments or suggestions concerning your approach. After this is done, you can request their assistance and, if possible, suggest several specific things they could do or contacts they could make for you.

Most people are flattered by requests for advice and enjoy assisting others. Consequently, these meetings should be among the easiest and most pleasant of your campaign. During these meetings, attempt to guide your contacts into being as specific as possible, particularly in regard to the ways in which they might help you or the people and companies to whom they might introduce you. Write down the names of these companies and individuals. If a contact suggests that you get in touch with another party, ask that he or she call to introduce you first.

Where it is impossible for you to meet personally with individuals on your contacts list, call them and briefly review the same information discussed above. End the conversation by telling them that you will send a copy of your resume and a description of your objectives.

In any case, make it easy for your contacts to assist you. Arm them with the information they need to consider specific possibilities, to discuss your qualifications and objectives with others, and to supply prospects with your past history of accomplishments. Even your closest business friends can do little with a request such as, "I'm looking for a job. Will you help?" They need to know specifically what you are looking for and why.

USE OF THE RESUME

Your resume should be given to each of your personal contacts. When you meet with them, you may leave one or more copies just prior to ending your conversation. If you prefer, tell them you will mail the resume. Then enclose it with your confirming letter.

In no case should you begin this or any other interview by giving out your resume. A meeting that starts with a resume can be awkward. Frequently you find yourself sitting with nothing to do as your contact reads the resume. Your obvious discomfort is likely to prompt your contact to read the resume rapidly and not give it the proper attention. This may be the only time he or she will read the resume.

In addition to this, a resume given out prior to a conversation can too easily become a crutch for both parties. As your contact continually refers to the resume, the conversation becomes overly structured and dwells excessively on your past instead of your future.

When the resume is given to your contact at the end of an interview, it is appropriate to request that it be read with care and to offer additional copies. The response to this offer may indicate your contact's willingness and ability to help.

In the hands of a personal contact, your resume becomes a positive instrument. When passing it on to potentially interested individuals, your contact will do so with a personal note or comment about you and about his or her interest in your background and abilities. The recipient will then search for reasons behind this recommendation as he or she reads the resume, all the while looking for your strengths rather than for your weaknesses.

FOLLOW-UP AND WRITTEN CONFIRMATION

Following the cardinal rule of this jobsearch manual, all telephone conversations and meetings with personal contacts should be confirmed by letter. You expect their help on a voluntary basis. This help is not a part of their job or daily routine. The confirming letter will be a written reminder of your conversation and their offer of assistance.

These letters usually contain three or four short paragraphs. The first should thank your contact for his or her time and offer of assistance. The second reviews your job objectives. In an optional third paragraph you may mention several of your strengths and list specific accomplishments that relate to your objectives. The final paragraph contains a statement of the expected follow-up and, if appropriate, a personal note. Two examples of such letters appear in the workbook (#29, #30).

After these letters and other correspondence with your personal contacts are filed in your notebook, it is advisable to underline in red and transfer to your "To Do" list any follow-up expected of you. This follow-up must then be performed on a timely basis. If you have indicated that you will check back with your contact after two weeks, do this within several days of the end of the second week. If your contact has suggested that you call another individual, do so and advise him or her of the results of this effort by phone or in a note.

Your personal contacts are important in your jobsearch campaign. Treat them with consideration; keep them advised of your progress, particularly regarding opportunities to which they introduce you.

COURTESY MEETINGS

One danger in using personal contacts is that you will become trapped in a long series of courtesy meetings. On occasion a friend with a genuine desire to help will request that you contact a business associate who does not represent a potential opportunity. This person will meet with you out of a sense of obligation to your mutual friend and may then send you to another uninterested party. These meetings can easily pyramid, resulting in a waste of valuable time.

The problem with such meetings is ascertaining in advance whether an opportunity exists. If you find that interviews of this type are absorbing an excessive amount of time, you may wish to mail a resume prior to setting up a meeting. This can be done by phoning the party and mentioning that you were referred to him or her by your mutual friend. You then outline the objectives of your jobsearch and offer to forward a copy of your resume for review, adding, "I'll contact you after you've had an opportunity to read it." Send your resume with a cover letter confirming your conversation, outlining your job objectives, stating several of your accomplishments, and indicating that you will call again later. Such a letter will be followed by a request for a personal meeting only if an opportunity does in fact exist.

Look at the example of this type of letter (#31). In this as in similar letters, the request for an interview is direct and without qualifications. If the interview is not appropriate, you will be told. Do not attempt to second-guess the interest of the other party or give that person any indication that a meeting may not be warranted.

CHAPTER 10

ANSWERING HELP WANTED ADVERTISEMENTS

Help wanted advertisements represent a good source of potential job opportunities. Because of the extent of their use and the volume of replies, however, you must answer numerous ads in order to generate any responses. Nevertheless, they should not be neglected. Using your accomplishments list and a basic form letter will enable you to answer ads with a minimum of effort.

Help wanted advertisements are placed by two primary sources. The first is by companies conducting their own personnel searches, showing their names and addresses or simply post office box numbers without company identification (called blind box numbers). The second is by employment agencies that list positions with companies by whom they have been retained. These are also placed with both blind box numbers and the name and address of the agency.

Occasionally, employment agencies will list fictitious positions in an effort to collect fresh resumes for their files. Although you cannot entirely avoid responding to such ads, your method of response can frustrate the objective of the agency and prevent an unwanted broadcast of your resume.

SOURCES OF ADS

One of the best sources of classified advertisements for most job campaigns is trade magazines. On the basis of your initial review of information sources, you should have already subscribed to any of these that are suitable. If you requested several editions prior to your subscription date, you will now have a backlog of advertisements that fall within your job targets.

Also, get appropriate city newspapers and obtain access to the Tuesday and Wednesday editions of *The Wall Street Journal*. Your contacts with national associations and college placement offices may have supplied you with additional listings of available positions.

If you have not already done so, carefully review all these advertisement sources. Read each ad and compare those of interest with your objectives and targets. Cut out the ads you intend to answer and note the name of the publication of each.

If publications you ordered have not yet arrived, call the publisher and expedite delivery. Explain your purpose and request that one or two recent copies be put in the mail to you immediately.

Answer all ads that you cut out, even those a month or two old. The company may not have found a suitable candidate. In addition, the fact that it is searching for additional employees may mean that the company is expanding or needs someone with your talents in another department or division.

Even if only a few ads are attractive to you, answer these and continue to examine all your sources throughout your campaign. Respond to the ads of interest until you have actually accepted a new position.

CHOICE OF ADS

In answering help wanted advertisements, be both liberal and expansive. Answer any advertisement in which you have an interest, even if the interest is based on curiosity or a flight of fancy. If you are interested in a specific company, answer its ads even though you are not strongly interested in the position advertised.

You should have at least some of the qualifications requested in the advertisements you answer. Remember, however, that no job candidate will present the ideal background and experience for any position. For this reason the company will have to compromise in making a final choice. It may be sufficiently interested in you to hire you as a subordinate to the person who gets the advertised position. It might also expand the advertised position to include other responsibilities in order to hire you if you are more qualified than intended.

Do not worry about the pay scale mentioned in the advertisements. If the figure is too low, it will be open for negotiation. If you are qualified and are the person the company wants, it will not hesitate to pay you the salary in the advertisement even if it is substantially higher than your last salary level.

Answer ads in which you have any interest whatsoever and as many of these as you can find. Each may represent another potentially attractive opportunity.

REPLY LETTERS

All your responses to help wanted advertisements should take the form of a one-page letter without a resume. In rare instances, such as a situation with a long list of requirements, two pages may be needed. In no case is a third page warranted.

If a company's name is shown or if the information contained in the advertisement makes the company's identity obvious, your reply letter should be personally addressed. Unless someone else is specifically mentioned in the ad, address the letter to the head of the department or the corporation officer responsible for the position. If the advertised position is for a salesperson or a district sales manager, this officer would be the vice-president of sales. If the position is at the vice-presidential level, this person would be the president or chief executive officer of the firm.

For most medium-size and large national companies, the names of these officers are listed in the Dun & Bradstreet *Middle Market* and *Million Dollar* directories. For local companies, chamber of commerce directories will list the chief executive officers of each corporation. In addition, executives of competing or supplier firms will often have the names of company managers and department heads. Of course, the easiest method of acquiring the appropriate name is to simply call the company and explain to the telephone operator that you wish to address a letter to the head of the appropriate department. You will be given the name you want.

Unless specifically instructed in the help wanted advertisement to do so, you should avoid addressing the letter to the director of personnel or to a specific person in this department. A letter addressed to a person by name, however, is always more highly regarded than one addressed simply to a company or to an unnamed department head. If the ad asks that the letter be sent to the director of personnel and a name is not given, do some research and find it.

In all cases your letter should be accomplishments oriented. In addition, it must respond directly and specifically to the qualifications or requirements mentioned in the ad. Before drafting the letter, carefully review the entire ad and your accomplishments list. Underline the qualifications requested in the ad; then select the one accomplishment that most nearly corresponds to the qualifications or responsibilities of greatest importance to the position advertised. This accomplishment should be included in the opening sentence of your letter. The idea is to immediately attract the attention of the recipient and make him or her interested in reading the rest of the letter.

The second sentence explains your reason for writing. It should refer to the advertisement and lead into a further listing of your accomplishments.

Then pick out four or five accomplishments that also relate to the position and the specific qualifications. List these with a double space between each accomplishment. If appropriate, a qualification mentioned in the ad can be repeated immediately before the accomplishment that responds to it. If necessary, rewrite the descriptions of your accomplishments to make them more responsive to the ad. It is usually wise to mention the names of companies that have employed you. This adds credibility to your accomplishments.

The next one- or two-sentence paragraph of your letter should contain just enough biographical information to put the reader's mind at ease about you. This should include some reference that indicates your age. If you do not wish to put your exact age, you might suggest it vaguely by referring to your years of experience or the ages of your children.

If your educational background is attractive or important to the advertised position, it should be cited. Do not mention education, however, if your lack of a specific degree requested in the advertisement is one of the few qualifications you lack.

You may wish to include the fact that you are married or are willing to travel or relocate. There should be no reference, however, to salary or any items relating to your personal objectives or job goals. Neither should there be the slightest indication that you might not be qualified for the job. The entire letter should point to the fact that you are.

The final paragraph of the letter should request a personal interview. It must be direct — to the point. You may indicate that you will be able to expand on your qualifications and background in the interview. Then ask for it.

End the letter with a statement indicating the follow-up expected and explaining how you can be reached. If the company's name is shown, maintain the initiative and state that you will phone a week to ten days after the letter is mailed. This is often an effective means of assuring that your letter is not discarded with little or no consideration. In addition, it will allow you to gather useful information about the job, plan your approach, and assess your chances. This will be important in your follow-up not only to this prospect but to subsequent opportunities as well.

A JOBSEARCH client making a phone call on an ad follow-up found himself talking to the secretary of a vice-president, who was out of town. In the process of asking the secretary a number of questions about the job, he noticed her accent and asked her where she came from. She came from Chicago. He told her that he had lived in Chicago for several years. At the end of the conversation, she told him she would put his letter on top of the pile with a note that he had called. Suddenly he found himself Number One among the hundreds of respondents.

Don't worry about bothering the company with your phone call. Had it wished, the company could have remained anonymous with a blind ad. Also, few candidates make such calls. It will demonstrate your interest and aggressive approach. You may even produce unusual and helpful results such as that mentioned above. Introduce yourself to the person you reach. Explain that you want to be sure your letter was received. Ask if the company needs more information. Ask how many replies to the ad were received, how many candidates the company intends to interview, and how and when the candidates will be chosen. Be sure to request an interview. If the interview is not granted, discuss the appropriate follow-up, all the while, if possible, keeping the initiative. State that you will call back again at an appropriate date.

Review the five examples of help wanted advertisements and letters responding to them (#32–#36). Pay particular attention to the format and order, the choice and listing of accomplishments, and the use of biographical data.

After you have answered a number of help wanted advertisements, it will become easy to develop a system to facilitate drafting these letters. Number the entries on your accomplishments list. Copy and then number sample paragraphs and sentences from your response letters. Use this information to develop a master list of paragraphs, sentences, and accomplishments. You can then compose a letter simply by indicating the numbers of appropriate items and have the letter typed directly from the master list. When doing this, however, review the wording to be certain it is appropriate for the specific advertisement. For most letters some sentences will have to be individually written.

File all your responses to help wanted advertisements in chronological order in the "Ad Answers" section of your notebook. Staple the advertisement in the upper right-hand corner of the letter.

When you receive a telephone call in response to one of these letters, explain that you answered several advertisements and ask to which the call refers. This will allow you to find the appropriate letter and have it and the advertisement in hand before starting the conversation.

Do not attempt to carry on a conversation of this type without having these copies. If you cannot find them immediately, say you would like to return the call in a few minutes when it would be more convenient for you. These calls are too important to waste. Having all the appropriate information available will allow you to respond more readily to the caller's questions and to elaborate on your accomplishments without excessive repetition.

REQUEST FOR RESUME AND SALARY INFORMATION

Most help wanted advertisements larger than single-column line ads request that a resume be sent. Ignore this request. The company placing the ad wants to get the maximum information about each candidate in order to facilitate its screening process. Your interest, on the other hand, is to provide the company with only enough information to provoke an interview. You cannot tailor your resume to the specific requirements of each advertisement. In addition, your resume may include information that the company would consider negative. The letters described above do not have these drawbacks. They are written and phrased for each individual ad.

In some advertisements the request for a resume is emphatic. The ad may state that you will not be considered if you do not send a resume. In such cases, mention in your reply letter that you do not have a current resume available. The company can easily assume you are not actively seeking new employment but responded to its advertisement because of its particular interest to you. Such an assumption can frequently work to your advantage.

Many help wanted advertisements also request your salary history or an indication of your desired salary. As with the resume, this request should be ignored. In cases where the request is emphatic, you may wish to include a sentence stating that your salary requirements are open and will depend on a more complete definition of the job, the responsibilities, and the potential.

There is one exception to this. When answering an ad for a federal government position or a job with a quasi-government agency, you should respond to a salary request. Salaries for these positions are not open to as much negotiation as positions in private industry, and the screening process for ad responses is more rigid. Do not give your salary history, but state an acceptable salary range using the government salary scale code. The range for the position and the appropriate code numbers can be determined by calling your local government information office or the agency that placed the ad.

RESPONSE TO EXPECT

When answering large display advertisements in national publications for positions of management responsibility, your rate of response can be as low as 1 to 3 percent. When answering local advertisements requesting specific technical expertise that is in high demand, your rate of response can be as high as 100 percent. These are the extremes, with the lower rates of response occurring more often. The point is that you should answer as many help wanted advertisements as practical and then expect a response rate of only a few percentage points.

A company's answer can come in the form of either a telephone call or a letter. Letters will express a polite refusal, a request for additional information, or a request for you to call to set up an interview.

Should additional information be requested, respond immediately and supply the information even if it includes a resume or salary history. In these instances, your letter will have attracted sufficient attention to cast your resume in a more positive light. Send it with a covering letter expressing your interest in the position, referring to accomplishments in your resume that reinforce your qualifications and requesting a personal interview. Review the ad and your original response to it before writing your cover letter.

If salary history or information is also requested, include this in your letter of transmittal (see #37). For desired salary, always state a range and emphasize that your salary requirements would depend on a number of factors that could best be discussed in a personal interview. Also, review Chapter 12 of this jobsearch manual before responding.

If the only request made is for salary information, respond by telephone. This will allow you to ask pertinent questions and also explain your salary range and the importance of other aspects of the job in establishing a final salary. You can then ask for an interview to discuss this matter in more detail.

Most telephone replies will be to set up a personal interview. In some instances the caller may wish to discuss several matters concerning the job and your background. This may constitute an almost complete job interview by telephone. Such calls are discussed in more detail in Chapter 14. Respond to all questions asked, while also indicating your desire to meet personally with the caller. You can sell yourself better in a meeting than by telephone and should make every effort to set up the interview.

SITUATION WANTED ADVERTISEMENTS

Most help wanted classified sections of newspapers and trade journals include situations wanted columns. These are advertisements placed by individuals seeking employment. They are a waste of money, as they generally elicit responses only from companies or organizations that wish to sell you a service or some franchise scheme.

The individuals and companies you wish to reach in your jobsearch campaign do not read situations wanted advertisements. If they are read by companies at all, the task is delegated to junior members of the personnel department, people whom you specifically want to avoid. In addition, a short advertisement cannot possibly include sufficient information and accomplishments to seriously interest a potential employer. Your approach must be more direct and more thorough than such an ad allows.

CHAPTER 11

MAIL MARKETING
CAMPAIGN

One of the most effective methods of finding job opportunities is a massive mail marketing campaign. Although it sometimes surprised us, over 80 percent of JOBSEARCH clients secured their jobs through their mail campaigns. This direct contact with executives in a large number of firms uncovers job opportunities for positions that are not advertised and would frequently never be advertised. On occasion companies were interested in these letters from our clients when no vacancies existed. The resulting interviews convinced the companies to create new positions in order to get our clients into their organizations.

Executives in business and in other organizations plan months ahead for additions to or changes in key personnel. A growing organization may plan to add a department or divide one department into two sections, thereby creating the need for a new department head. It may plan to open a new territory, thus creating the need for additional salespeople and sales managers, or it may recognize a weakness in its organization and decide that a change in personnel is warranted.

A large truck-body manufacturer acquired three other divisions during the past five years. Although the organization had a corporate staff of only nine, every discipline was covered except personnel. At about the time the company started discussing its needs in this area, an industrial relations manager came to JOBSEARCH. Neither he nor this company knew of each other, but the company was on Ed's mailing list. After two interviews Ed had the corporate human resources position he wanted. Interestingly, six months before coming to JOBSEARCH, Ed sent resumes to over 400 executive recruiters resulting in interviews with only two companies. Neither had the job he wanted.

Situations similar to those described above represent potential job opportunities for you. If an unexpected letter arrives from a candidate who appears qualified for one of these future positions, that person will be interviewed. If you then sell yourself as the one to fill the future vacancy or solve the impending problem, you will be hired even though such a move might be considered premature.

Hiring good people is a difficult, time-consuming, and expensive process. When a well-qualified candidate appears, a company would rather hire him or her than advertise for, screen, and interview applicants or pay an agency or recruiter to perform only a portion of this work. Your job is to find the companies that might need you to fill a position of this type. A mail marketing campaign can help do this.

SOURCES OF INFORMATION

One of the most important items of information for a direct mail campaign is the name of the appropriate recipient for each letter. Just as a letter addressed to "resident" is frequently discarded unopened, a letter addressed to a company without the name of a specific individual seldom finds its way to the appropriate person. Your objective is to have your letter read by a company executive who would be interested in you and also have the authority to hire you if he or she wished to do so. Your source of information must provide the name of this person.

In addition to these names, the information you use must disclose enough about the firm — its size and its products or services — to allow you to evaluate your interest in working there. You must also be able to determine the company's potential interest in someone of your experience or someone requiring your level of compensation. A manufacturing firm employing 25 people cannot afford to hire a vice-president and treasurer earning $35,000 a year. On the other hand, you may prefer working for a smaller organization where you would be called upon to exercise a broader range of responsibilities. To the extent possible, your sources of information must allow you to exercise these judgments.

For each of your job targets, find a listing of appropriate companies that includes as much of the following information as possible:

> Name and address of the company
> Name of the chief executive officer
> Names of other officers in the corporation
> Description of the firm's products or services
> An indication of the firm's size
> Number and location of divisions and subsidiaries

A number of suitable information sources was mentioned in the preliminary work section of this jobsearch manual. If you have visited your public library and contacted appropriate chambers of commerce and other organizations, you should be ready to make specific choices concerning these sources. You will find that the chamber of commerce publications are excellent for a jobsearch campaign limited to a single or a few specific geographical areas. For a broader search, the Dun & Bradstreet *Million Dollar Directory* and *Middle Market Directory* are excellent. For specific industries or targets outside of industry, trade association publications or membership lists should be investigated.

Other possible sources of information can be found in the *Encyclopedia of Business Information Sources* and the *Guide to American Directories* (see #9 in the jobsearch workbook). If your library does not have the directories you need, it may order them for you. Some may be inexpensive enough for you to order yourself.

To give you some idea of the specialized directories available, *The Advertiser's Red Book* lists most agencies in the United States. In addition to the information described above, the book also lists each agency's major clients. The *Martindale-Hubbel Law Directory* provides the names of all private lawyers and law firms. The *Polk Bank Directory* includes information needed to choose and contact these financial institutions.

Vast information is available on American business and industry. It may take imagination and effort to find what you need, but it can be done. Ask for help at your library. Call association offices; talk to executives and others in industries that interest you. Tell them what you are doing, what information you need, and why. From these contacts you will find one or more directories or lists that suit your purpose.

CHOOSING TARGET FIRMS

When choosing specific firms to include in your mailing, match the industry, size, and geographical areas of your job targets as closely as possible. Once again, however, be liberal in your choices. It is better to list too many firms than too few.

When your list is complete, most of the work is done. The cost of typing and mailing additional letters is minimal. For these reasons you should include between 300 and 500 companies on your list. Except in special circumstances, if your initial list is not at least this long, expand it. Go back and review your target definitions. Expand them in one or more areas even though these might rank lower in your job preferences. Using these expanded targets, review your information sources and increase the number of entries on your mailing list.

Throughout this process you will find it convenient to keep your written target definitions in front of you. Thus, you can refer to them as you review information on companies and information from various sources.

When making up your mailing list, do not neglect medium-size and small companies. Mailing lists are available commercially for the top 1,000 U.S. firms. These companies are therefore inundated with letters and resumes—mostly addressed to the president or chief executive officer. When listing these firms, avoid the president; try to address an appropriate vice-president. The majority of your list should consist of firms that are not in this group. If you use the Dun & Bradstreet directories, take a large proportion of the names, if not the majority of them, out of the *Middle Market Directory*. Regardless of your qualifications, write to firms where you will not be in competition with numerous other job seekers.

If your campaign is directed toward one city, be particularly thorough in your choice of companies. Check your mailing lists from the chamber of commerce and other directories against the telephone Yellow Pages for that city. Be sure to include manufacturers' representatives firms, consulting firms, and other organizations in the city that might be interested in you or know of companies that would be.

WHOM TO ADDRESS

The recipient of your letter should be the individual in the company to whom you would report if hired. The next best choice is the person to whom that individual reports. One of these people will usually be an officer of the company or the head of a department. In any case, it is preferable to address the letter to the lowest-placed executive holding responsibility over the position for which you are applying.

This is the individual most interested in having strong people working with him or her. This person will readily identify with your accomplishments and relate them to his or her daily problems. In addition, this person will know of vacancies or weaknesses in his or her department that may not be known to higher officials.

Many sources of information list only a single name for each company, usually that of the president. Where other officers' names would be difficult to obtain, addressing the letter to the chief executive is both sufficient and appropriate. This is always preferable to addressing an unnamed department head. You should, however, attempt to find a more precise target. *Who's Who in Business and Finance* will include some names that are not shown in company directories. For companies in which you are most interested, call the office and get the information you want.

If for certain companies you are forced to use the Yellow Pages or other directories that do not list names, as a last resort address your letter to the appropriate department head with the salutation, "Dear Sir." This is better than not contacting the firm at all.

MAILING LISTS

You should make up a separate mailing list for each of your job targets. Usually these will have enough dissimilarities to require some differences in the wording of your marketing letters. Each letter will have to be given to the autotyping service with the list of names and addresses that corresponds to it.

Lists must be written legibly and should contain the addresses with the same information and in the same format as will appear on the envelope. Included are:

> The name of the individual
> The title of the individual
> The name of the company
> The street address
> The city, state, and zip code

If you plan to follow up any of your marketing letters with a telephone call, also list the telephone number.

If your mailing list comes from a directory you own, it is not necessary to copy out all the names and addresses by hand. Simply put a bracket around the appropriate company name, using a red pen, and underline the name and title of the recipient.

Because you will not keep copies of each autotyped letter, it is advisable to file a copy of each mailing list at the end of the "Mail Campaign" section of your notebook. If you have not written out the addresses, you can ask the autotyping service to prepare a list as it types the letters. The names and addresses should all be placed on the left-hand side of the paper. The right-hand side can then be used for notations of response and required follow-up. Any subsequent follow-up correspondence, notes, and records should be grouped by company and filed in the "Prospects" section of your notebook.

For your mail marketing campaign, it is important that all your letters are mailed on the same day. When you are performing the laborious task of handcopying your mailing lists, you may want to spread out the job by doing one list or section each week, then mailing these letters and continuing the effort week by week. However, this is not advisable. One objective of your jobsearch campaign is to secure multiple job offers simultaneously. If your mailing period is extended, you may find yourself in initial interviews with one firm while you are in final negotiations with another.

THE MARKETING LETTER

As was the case with your responses to help wanted advertisements, send your mail marketing letter without a resume. The letter for each job target should be carefully organized and worded to respond to the probable interest of the recipient. It must also contain a specific statement of your immediate job objective.

Even if you have had a broad range of experience, each letter must be directed toward one job target that is well defined. It should be a job title or job description familiar to the recipient and one that is realistic. Indicating that you will accept any of several positions will dissipate the effect of your letter and severely lessen your rate of response. Business managers have specific, not general, problems. Job responsibilities are usually well defined even for high-level positions. People are hired to solve these special problems and exercise the responsibilities of one job. They are not hired to motivate their subordinates in a general sense, or to exercise broad responsibilities encompassing several departmental functions.

Your letter should not allude to unanswered questions concerning you or your career. Do not include any item that could be construed as negative or interpreted as a weakness. Do not refer to any aspect of your career that is not self-explanatory. All sentences in this letter should be short and to the point. Eliminate any extraneous words. Use as few adjectives as possible, and do not include gratuitous references to yourself.

Study the five examples of marketing letters (#38–#42), paying particular attention to the following descriptions of layout and wording:

Date. All letters should show the date on which they will be mailed. Check with the autotyping service you intend to use about its workload and the time required to complete the letters. Add several days to this to give yourself time to sign and prepare the letters. Then date them, usually for the following Thursday or Friday. Before deciding on a date, read the section in this chapter on "When to Mail."

Address. The address on both the letter and the envelope should show the name and title of the recipient, the company name, its address, and the zip code. Use abbreviations for Company (Co.) or Incorporated (Inc.) only if that designation is so given in your source of information. Use no other abbreviations in the address.

Salutation. The salutation should read "Dear Mr. _____," showing the last name of the recipient. Do not use the salutation "Dear Sir" or "Gentlemen." If the recipient is a woman, the form "Ms." is now usually preferable except in situations where the person has specified either "Mrs." or "Miss."

The first sentence. Your first sentence should attract the attention of the reader. As with your responses to advertisements, it should include the single accomplishment of your career most indicative of your competence in the targeted job. In most cases this sentence should contain a reference to the title you held at the time of the accomplishment. It should also contain some reference to the company either by name—if that would be known to the recipient—or by definition of its industry and size. Before writing this sentence, review your accomplishments list again. Write several drafts. Study each of them, placing yourself in the position of the reader, and then choose the most effective. If possible, the accomplishment used should be one that is quantified with numbers and has a direct relation to the profitability or success of the organization for which you worked. This is the most important sentence of the entire letter. Write it with care.

The second sentence. The second sentence acts as a bridge between your opening statement and the remainder of your letter. It should indicate why you are writing to the reader. It should also state that you might respond to one of the reader's needs or help solve a problem he or she has. Finally, it should introduce a listing of your accomplishments. Study the second sentences in the sample letters in the workbook. Again, write several drafts of your letters. Check each to be certain it responds to the above criteria.

Accomplishments. In this section list an additional four or five accomplishments that best relate to your job target. Each should be complete, stating what you did and the results of your actions. Wherever possible, the accomplishments should be quantified. Use of the word "I" is optional. Base this decision on your personal preference and the number of times the word is used in other parts of the letter, but do not start your description of each accomplishment with "I."

The third paragraph. This should contain biographical information similar in scope and intent to that used in your advertisement response. If the second sentence of your letter is not sufficiently descriptive of the job you seek, or if you wish to qualify your job objectives, add an appropriate sentence at this point in the letter. It should relate, however, only to the job you seek. Do not include any reference to your personal objectives or career goals. Do not state that you are looking for a position that would use your talents to the maximum extent, or that you want to find a challenge or a pleasant working atmosphere.

The final paragraph. The final paragraph should state your desire for a personal interview and whether you expect to be contacted by the company or plan to phone it. For a short list of companies or those you are particularly interested in, it is wise to say you will phone. Then block out one or two days and telephone as many contacts as possible, setting up as many interviews as you can.

If your search is directed toward one or two cities remote from your current home, it is particularly effective to state that you plan to be in the city during a specified period, usually three to five days about three weeks to a month after your mailing. You will then have to pay for the trip yourself, but you will find companies responding that would otherwise not have done so. Then make the best possible use of your time in that area for interviews, follow-up, and other local contacts that might produce job leads.

USE OF AUTOTYPING

Once you have completed the final draft of each of your sales letters, they should be typed with a sample name and address, all in the identical format, spacing, and line length that you want the autotypist to use. Indicate on each letter the target for which it is intended. These typed drafts and each mailing list should be taken to the autotypist and reviewed in detail. Pay particular attention to spelling, punctuation, and grammar.

The autotypist will prepare your letters and envelopes and, if you have requested it, a copy of the mailing list. You will then need to sign each of the letters and make sure you place each in the correct envelope. When stamped, the envelopes will be ready for mailing on the date indicated in the enclosed letter.

WHEN TO MAIL

The job market is somewhat seasonal and is also affected by holidays and vacation periods. The market is most favorable just after the first of January when business people are beginning to act on their planning for the year. It falls off slightly during the summer vacation period, increases in the fall, and declines again with the approach of Thanksgiving and the Christmas holiday season.

For most jobsearch campaigns you will have neither the luxury of time nor the inclination to delay your mailing for several months as you wait out summer vacations. Furthermore, the drop in hiring activity during this period is not sufficient to warrant such a wait. It is advisable, however, not to mail your letters during the period from the first week before Thanksgiving to the first week after New Year's Day. The letters should definitely not be mailed during the period from December 15 through January 5. Also, avoid mailing your letters during the week of any holiday, particularly if the holiday results in a long weekend.

It is best if your letter arrives on a Monday or Tuesday. This allows the recipient time during the week to respond without the break of a weekend. For this reason you should date your local letters on a Friday and put them in the mail on either Saturday or Sunday. Date and mail out-of-state letters one day prior to doing so for local letters.

RESPONSE TO EXPECT

The first responses to your mail campaign will come in the form of telephone calls. These will all be positive indications of interest and will usually come within ten days of your mailing. A discussion of these calls is included in Chapter 14, "Telephone Interviews."

Following receipt of these initial calls, you will begin to receive letters. The total response to your mailing will greatly exceed that of your replies to help wanted advertisements. Usually it will be over 25 percent. A large portion of business firms will answer a personal letter even though the replies are negative. The great majority of the letters you receive, therefore, will be polite refusals. Do not become discouraged by the volume of rejections. They are a normal and expected part of any large direct mailing.

We had a JOBSEARCH client who sent out as few as 157 letters that resulted in 17 interviews and other clients who sent out as many as 600 letters in three successive mailings that resulted in only one interview. In every case, however, the jobs secured resulted from the direct mail campaigns.

Among your responses, some letters will be positive. Either they will request that you call to set up an interview or that you send a resume or other information, or they will show interest but be vague concerning follow-up or the availability of an opening. These should all be answered in the same manner as described in the section "Response to Expect" in Chapter 10.

If the additional information requested is to be given on an employment application, fill out the form even though it may be designed for use by secretaries and clerks. Mail it back with a cover letter expressing your interest in the job. If the application does not adequately cover your experience and accomplishments, consider attaching a copy of your resume. Even if you do this, fill out the application completely. Where negative information is required, such as the reasons for past job changes, be truthful but positive. Show that you are cooperative and follow instructions. Follow the sample letter of this type (#43).

Responses to the mail campaigns of our JOBSEARCH clients came as much as three months after the letters were mailed. Many companies keep such letters pending future openings or changes. In large companies the letter may be circulated for some time between divisions and subsidiaries. In most cases, however, you will have received most—if not all—of your responses one month after your mailing.

CHAPTER 12

OTHER CONTACTS

So far this jobsearch manual has concentrated on the three most effective methods of finding job opportunities—personal contacts, answering help wanted advertisements, and conducting a direct mail marketing campaign. In most job campaigns there are other avenues that can and should be explored. These consist primarily of contacts with other organizations or individuals that can often be of help. The effectiveness of these contacts will vary widely depending on your job targets and individual circumstances. It is not suggested that you make all these contacts. Review them. Do enough research to determine which might be helpful, and proceed with those that appear most attractive to your situation.

Just as with your personal contacts, it will be appropriate to give your resume to all the contacts that will be discussed in this chapter. These individuals would not normally represent organizations with job opportunities for you; instead, they can be a conduit to these opportunities. When passing your resume on to potentially interested parties, they will generally include their own positive comments.

EMPLOYMENT AGENCIES

For most jobsearch campaigns, employment agencies will be of little assistance. In some cases they may even be detrimental. These agencies are retained by companies to find applicants for specific job vacancies. Applicants are subsequently screened and interviewed by the company. If one of them is hired, the employment agency is paid a commission ranging from 7½ to 15 percent of the first year's salary. For most jobs at the supervisory level or above, this commission is paid by the company. For lower-level jobs, the fee is frequently paid by the job seeker.

The employment agency's incentive is to provide as many applicants as possible for any vacancy. It has little incentive to do substantial preliminary screening of candidates. It has virtually no incentive to assist persons seeking employment by doing anything except distributing their resumes and sending them on as many interviews as they might accept. In your jobsearch campaign, these interviews can be time consuming. Too frequently they are for jobs that match neither your targets nor your career goals. In addition, you do not want your resume distributed to a large number of firms, many of which you might contact yourself in a more appropriate manner.

In spite of these negative possibilities, employment agencies can be of use in some campaigns. If you are conducting a geographically dispersed search in a narrow field, you may find there are employment agencies that specialize in your particular field. If you are conducting a campaign in one or more specific cities and are looking for a lower-level supervisory or technical job at $12,000 to $20,000 per year, there are usually one or two employment agencies in each city that may be helpful. In any case, employment agencies must be chosen with care.

Register with no more than two or three agencies for any specialty or in any city. If you are looking in a specialized field, employment agencies whose efforts are concentrated in your profession will be listed in small display ads in the help wanted sections of trade journals. If you find more than two agencies listed, phone and talk to the chief executive. Inquire about the number of people in your specialty that the agency places per year and ask about other fields that the agency covers. Request a listing of ten companies by whom the agency has been retained in the past six months. From answers to these questions you should be able to choose the two or three agencies that would be most effective for your campaign.

For a local campaign, choosing employment agencies is more difficult. Of the large number available, only a few will do substantive work with management-level personnel. Phone the directors of personnel of four or five large companies in your target city. Ask them for the names of employment agencies and the individuals in these agencies whom they use for middle-level management positions. Define what your specific targets are, and explain your reason for asking.

From these conversations, you should be able to determine which agencies would be most appropriate for your search. Then register with them. To do this, phone the agency and ask for the name of the chief executive or the manager. This is the person with whom you should register.

If the agency is local, arrange a personal meeting with this person. During the interview, you must be as specific as possible. Define your job targets. Explain the methods you are using in your jobsearch, and ask the agency executive to define how he or she anticipates helping you. You must request that your resume not be mailed out for jobs that do not match your targets. Also, explain that you do not want your resume sent to firms that have not registered an appropriate vacancy with the agency. Specify a minimum salary on the high side of your range and state that you would prefer that this subject not be discussed with a potential employer.

At the conclusion of this meeting, give the agency executive one copy of your resume. Immediately following the meeting, write a polite but strong confirming letter reviewing each of the points covered in your conversation.

For distant employment agencies, call the manager or chief executive and introduce yourself. Briefly explain the reason for your call and ask if it would be appropriate for you to register with the agency. Then confirm the call with a letter and resume. As in a personal meeting, the letter must be specific regarding your targets and the use of your resume by the agency. Look over the sample letter (#44). With minor modifications, this same letter can be used as the confirming letter for a meeting with an agency.

When registering with employment agencies for positions other than low-level jobs, do not fill out application forms. These forms are primarily designed for use by clerks and office staff. They require information irrelevant to your job campaign as well as information that you might not want divulged to a prospective employer. If you are requested to fill out such an application, explain politely that it is not appropriate to your search. If further demands are made, register with another agency. Also, avoid signing contracts that might bind you to paying the agency a fee or might result in fee disputes if you secure a job through other contacts with a firm the agency suggested.

EXECUTIVE RECRUITERS

Executive recruiters are firms or individuals who take on employee searches for high-level positions. In most cases they look for a person with direct experience in their client's industry and attempt to steal such a person from another firm. It is because of this practice that executive recruiters have attracted the nicknames "headhunters" and "body snatchers." Their fees are 25 percent or more of the first year's salary and are always paid by the company. Because of these high fees, they are usually retained only by large and medium-size companies.

Although most executive recruiters are looking for specialized talent at any given moment, they have high-level contacts with a large number of firms. If you are conducting a national search for a position at the district manager, general manager, vice-president, or president level with a company employing more than 500 people, you should register with executive recruiters.

The American Management Associations (AMA) publishes a list of these firms. It includes each firm's address, its telephone number, the kinds of positions it handles, the minimum salary of each position, and the firm's willingness to review resumes and interview candidates on an unsolicited basis. There is also an alphabetical code indicating the type of services provided. Individuals' names are not given; however, it is sufficient in this case to address a letter to the firm only.

In choosing firms with which to register, use only those providing executive search, code "A" in the AMA list. Do not use licensed personnel agencies, code "D," unless they are appropriate as discussed in the section on agencies elsewhere in this chapter. Otherwise, firms can be chosen according to the kinds of positions they handle and the location of their offices. Register with between 70 and 100 firms by using an autotyped letter. It should include a short summary of your qualifications and state your job objectives along with any limitations or restrictions—such as geographical location. Salary should be mentioned in the same manner as it was in the letter to employment agencies. There is no risk that these firms will distribute your resume indiscriminately, and so this need not be discussed. Enclose one copy of your resume with the letter. Use the sample letter (#45) as a model.

COLLEGE PLACEMENT OFFICES

In your preliminary work you will have determined if there are appropriate college placement offices that will submit your resume to firms that have registered vacancies or subscribe to their listing service. For a job campaign covering a large geographical area, the placement office of your alma mater should be investigated. For a local campaign, register with all nearby colleges and universities that accept resumes from individuals who are not their alumni. Your cover letter should be personally addressed to the director of the placement office and should be similar in format and wording to that shown for executive recruiters.

TRADE ASSOCIATIONS

Some trade associations provide services similar to those of college placement offices. The Association of MBA Executives is an example. For $15 per month the Association will print a short summary of your background and job objectives in a booklet it submits to over 500 subscribing firms. On request, it will send the firm your complete resume.

Again, from your preliminary information sources and the *Encyclopedia of Associations,* find out which of these organizations might be of help. Register, using another letter similar to the one for executive recruiters.

ACCOUNTING FIRMS

Accounting firms are frequently in a unique position to know of vacancies in or points of weakness at the managerial levels of their clients' organizations. Because of this and their close relationship with their clients, many of the Big Eight and other large CPA firms in major cities have placement officers. If you are seeking a job at a high management level, it would be appropriate to call the major accounting firms in the city or cities in which you are concentrating your effort. Ask if they have a placement service or officer. Talk to the person in charge and follow the registration procedure indicated.

When you have a personal contact with a CPA firm, make sure he or she has a copy of your resume and knows of your search. Follow the procedure for other personal contacts.

For other local job campaigns, particularly those directed toward a job target in the financial area, register with the top 10 to 20 accounting firms, using an autotyped letter and resume. If possible, address the letter to the managing partner.

CHAMBERS OF COMMERCE

For campaigns concentrating in one or more major cities, advise the director of the local chamber of commerce of your availability and search. These persons are knowledgeable about the area, local businesses, and local business leaders. After determining the name of the appropriate individual, you can meet with or phone him or her and then send a letter and resume.

BANKS AND LAWYERS

Commercial loan officers of banks and lawyers specializing in corporate work on occasion know of job openings in their client firms. These persons, however, do not participate in the job market as actively as others mentioned above. For this reason, contact them only if you know them personally or have an introduction.

EMPLOYMENT CONFERENCES

From time to time advertisements for employment conferences appear in large-city newspapers. These are mass meetings designed to put job seekers and companies seeking employees into contact with one another. They are effective for individuals in technical, rather than management-level, positions. Even so, this can be a humiliating experience. You may find yourself in a group of from 500 to 1,000 job seekers all trying to arrange 10- to 15-minute interviews with overworked personnel representing 15 to 20 major corporations. This kind of atmosphere is seldom conducive to a discussion in which you can sell your talent and experience.

CHAPTER 13

SPECIAL SITUATIONS

Special situations occur in a jobsearch campaign when there are one or two specific companies or organizations for which you would like to work. You should have definite reasons for this preference. Perhaps you have been particularly impressed by the company's history or its method of doing business. You might have close friends who work there and would be willing to assist you. You may know that this company not only has a special need for your talent but also represents attractive potential for your career development.

John Fenner was one of our first JOBSEARCH clients. He wanted to join a new firm set up by three former colleagues. He was excited by their entrepreneurial spirit. After pursuing this as a "special situation," he moved into the new company and has since split off to form his own venture.

For whatever reasons, however, be sure your preference for the company merits the time and effort required to approach it as a separate target. In no case should you devote this amount of time to more than two or three companies.

IDENTIFYING SPECIAL SITUATIONS

The most important criterion for identifying a special situation is your reason for wanting to work with that company or organization. Beyond this, you must be able to secure information, preferably from both inside and outside the company, that will allow you to completely develop your case for employment. Finally, you must have physical access to the company to gather information and then to present your case.

Prior to starting your jobsearch campaign you might have several such companies in mind. You may uncover others during your search. In either case, pursuing these situations should be only one part of your overall jobsearch effort. Except in instances where you will be able to keep your current employment if you do not secure a job with one or two preselected firms, do not devote more than a portion of your jobsearch to special situations.

In most cases an entire jobsearch campaign will be successfully executed without any effort directed toward a single company. However, if you feel that several special situations offer attractive opportunities, gather preliminary information concerning the companies and complete the "special situation" form (#46).

COMPILING INFORMATION

In pursuing an individual company as a job opportunity, you need to secure two types of information. The first is a general but complete history and description of the firm, including the department, division, or subsidiary for which you want to work. The second is the information you will need to develop a thorough and convincing case for your employment. Both of these will involve substantial time, detailed research, and careful planning.

Regarding the company history, it should be accumulated and kept in outline form for your own use and reference. In the preliminary phase of gathering this information, do not divulge your reasons. You may explain to the people you consult that you are doing a study of the company, its industry, or its markets. With this explanation, most people will divulge a surprising extent of information about their company.

If the firm is publicly owned, get a copy of its latest annual report. The company will send this on request. You might also ask for copies of the annual reports for the previous five to ten years. From the Securities and Exchange Commission, 500 North Capitol Street, Washington, D.C. 20549, request the latest 10-K financial report on the company. This will include more complete financial data than are included in the published annual statement. Copies of the 10-K report are available to the public at a cost of about

10 cents per page, or around $5 to $10 each. They can be ordered with a letter addressed to the attention of "Public Reference." Request to be billed the correct amount when the report is sent.

Whether the company is publicly held or not, you can phone their public relations or administrative officer and request copies of all available recent news releases. Also, ask if a company history has been published, or if any other historical information is available to the public.

An officer of a bank can order a Dun & Bradstreet report on the company for you. This will provide information concerning the company's financial condition and credit rating. It includes a description of the products and services offered, a short history of the company, and biographical data on the principal owners or officers. These reports are available on private as well as publicly held companies. They are also available for companies with as few as one or two employees.

For large companies, go to the public library and look up the name of the company and the key words describing its products, its markets, or particular activities that interested you in the directories you have used in other parts of your jobsearch.

Be sure to include the *Business Periodicals Index*. This will give you sources of business magazine articles about the company, its markets, and its competitors. Order those you want from the publishers, or make copies of them from past issues in the library.

For local companies, look up these same items in the index of newspaper articles available at the main office of the paper. Finally, secure a listing of the officers and major department heads of the company or subsidiaries in which you are interested. If this is not available from published sources, phone the company's competitors and suppliers. Obtain any names that you cannot get in this manner by calling the company's telephone operator.

From the above data, write your outline history of the company. Pay particular attention to accumulating a concise record of gross annual sales, net profits, cost of goods sold, general administrative and sales expenses, total assets, total liabilities, stockholders' equity, and stock prices over the past ten-year period. You will find it convenient and instructive to draw graphs showing the movement for each of these important financial indices. Use this information to calculate, record, and graph the return on sales, the return on stockholders' equity, the ratio of total liabilities to net worth, the stock price to earnings ratio, and the ratio of current assets to current liabilities.

Additional financial data of a similar type relating to your specialty, division, or department should also be accumulated, recorded, and graphed. For example, if you are interested in research, determine the total research budget and calculate its ratio to sales and earnings. If you are interested in sales, separate total sales expense and compute its relation to sales and earnings.

In as complete a form as possible, draw an organization chart of the company and the department, division, or subsidiary for which you wish to work. Gather as much information as you can about the individuals on this chart. Write short biographical sketches of them. Include any personality traits mentioned by others.

All the above information should give you a good working knowledge of the company with particular emphasis on the area of your intended job.

DEVELOPING YOUR CASE

Once your history of the company is complete, start on the information you will need to develop the case for your employment. You will find it helpful to identify and cultivate within the company a close contact who can supply you with information. Because you will not want to divulge your objective prematurely, this contact must be developed with care. It should not be a person whom you might replace or whose performance you might criticize when presenting your case. The ideal contact would be on the same level as your desired position, but someone who would not feel threatened by your presence. It should be someone who has an interest in the same area of company activity as you have and, if possible, someone who might benefit from your presence. You will have to use your own judgment in deciding how much you can confide in this person and whether you should advise him or her of your objective.

In some cases an inside contact as intimate as that just described is impossible to secure. This should not deter you from pursuing a special situation. You will simply have to rely on other contacts, either inside or outside the company, and perhaps use data more incomplete than you wish.

In developing your case for employment, concentrate exclusively on the contribution you can make to the company. Do not mention your personal objectives, your career objectives, what the company might offer you, or the satisfaction you might gain from your contribution. Address yourself to a need the company has or should have. Demonstrate how your fulfilling this need will contribute to the performance or success of the organization. Finally, show from your past accomplishments how you are suited to fulfill this need, perform the required duties, and achieve the projected results.

Our client John Fenner, whose case was mentioned earlier in this manual, was an office manager for a construction company. When the new firm that eventually hired him had grown large enough to need and support his talents, he began to develop his approach. At that point he could readily show what he could bring to the organization.

You might, for instance, be a salesperson who could open a new market or market territory for the company. Use your accomplishments to demonstrate your knowledge and effectiveness in the new market. Relate the cost of developing this market to the expected profits that could result, and demonstrate how penetration of this new market will contribute to the continued sales growth and objectives of the company. If you are an engineer with particular experience in computer applications, demonstrate how these techniques might affect the scheduling and cost of the company's current engineering work. Relate the cost effectiveness of work you have performed in the past to the results expected for the prospective employer.

Your case should be developed fully in outline form for your own use. It should then be summarized in a concise, written report suitable for submission to the company.

INITIAL INTERVIEW

After the above work is completed, you will be ready to present your case for employment. Your initial contact should be with the person who has direct responsibility over the functions you intend to perform. That person should also have the authority to hire you.

In regard to your request for a job, the initial contact can be either direct or indirect. Use your own judgment in deciding which is more appropriate. For an indirect approach, you might present your case as an independent study or a portion of a larger study you are undertaking without any suggestion that you are seeking employment. The objective in this approach and the subsequent follow-up is to induce the prospective employer to originate the idea of hiring you.

Another indirect approach is to have your case presented initially by a third party. It is best if this person knows both you and the company representative you wish to contact. Depending on the situation and your intermediary's knowledge of you and your contact, this can vary from a simple introduction of the work you have done to a complete disclosure of your objectives. Make this decision and review with your intermediary his or her entire presentation.

In the direct approach, present your case and your request for employment simultaneously. In most instances the direct approach is preferable. It cannot be construed as a subterfuge. It eliminates the problem of explaining the reason for and extent of your investigation. It also eliminates the possibility that a job will never be discussed.

Even though you may disclose your objective, the purpose of this initial meeting is primarily to exchange information. You should not dwell on your desire for employment. Instead, concentrate on the company's needs, the methods of answering these needs, and the expected results. As an outsider who has developed his or her case without the benefit of complete access to company records, you should readily admit that your facts and assumptions may be incorrect.

Avoid being presumptuous and egotistical. No matter how thoroughly you have prepared your case, your contact knows more than you do about the company, its problems, and its objectives. Question your contact carefully. Delve into the areas of weakness in your plan. Ask your contact if more study or further consideration of additional information may be warranted. Your intent is to stimulate the imagination and curiosity of your contact. Although you should not expect an offer in this first meeting, you do not want a refusal either.

Before going to this meeting, review Chapter 15 of this jobsearch manual. Pay particular attention to the sections "Managing the Interview" and "Questions to Ask."

If, at the end of this initial meeting, your contact is convinced that your plan may have merit and has agreed to provide you with additional information to develop your assumptions and projections, you will have succeeded.

Confirm this meeting with a letter. Thank your contact for his or her time and interest. Describe the work you intend to do as a result of the interview. State the expected follow-up and its timing. Use the sample letter (#47) as a model.

SOLICITING A JOB OFFER

In subsequent interviews, continue to expand both your case and the idea that you are the best candidate to produce the projected results for the company. Gradually become more aggressive on this latter point until you receive a job offer or, at an appropriate time, request employment and instigate negotiations yourself.

Do not accept an initial refusal. Ask instead if you can study the question further. Review your interest in the company. Be aggressive about the contribution you can make to the profits and success of the organization. Once again, until your contact has accepted the idea of your employment and you are negotiating for your position, do not mention benefits that might accrue to you or conditions that you might wish to impose.

If you receive a definite refusal, it will be difficult to appeal to a higher authority in the company without requesting permission to do so from your initial contact. You should, however, make this request. You might also explore with your contact other divisions in the company that might be interested in your proposal. In addition, request information about or introductions to competitors or other companies with a possible interest. If you have done your work thoroughly and have made a convincing case, you might find a more receptive audience in a company completely unknown to you.

Continue to pursue your interest until you have reached a successful conclusion or have investigated every possible approach. If your facts are right, if your case is convincing, and if you sell yourself, you will succeed.

WORKING FOR YOURSELF

When you have decided to make a job change, investigate all possibilities. One of these is working for yourself. If you have had an urge to try this, now may be an opportune time for some preliminary investigations. This can be done at the same time you conduct your jobsearch campaign. In addition, the techniques explained in this jobsearch manual can be used as tools for this investigation with some types of businesses.

An example of this is working for yourself as a manufacturer's representative. Two letters (#48 and #49) were sent out in direct mailings at the same time that other letters were sent to larger firms concerning a job.

When considering this possibility, examine your intent carefully. If working for yourself is a way out of possible failure in the job market, do not try it. Starting a new business is risky, difficult, and time consuming. You must forgo much of your family life to spend time on the problems of inadequate capitalization, workforce, and recognition in the marketplace. Review your career goals. If substantial equity in the future is not one of them, assess your entrepreneurial spirit. If it is not real, running your own business is a prescription for disaster.

If, on the other hand, you must try it at least once in your life, now may be the time. Review your financial resources and possible avenues for raising additional capital. Make sure you study the business thoroughly and are ready to support both your family and the future business while you make substantial sacrifices and fight the high risk of failure. Over 75 percent of new businesses fail within the first few years, most because of inadequate capitalization. Success, however, can be satisfying and lucrative. Make certain the risk is worth the potential gain.

PART THREE

SELLING YOURSELF

CHAPTER 14

TELEPHONE INTERVIEWS

A wide audience of potential employers is now aware of your career accomplishments and job objectives. Companies and organizations with an interest in you will begin making their initial contacts. The first of these will be telephone calls. Virtually without exception they will be positive. Companies that do not wish to consider hiring you will respond by letter if they respond at all. For this reason you must be prepared to accept these calls and stimulate the initial interest of the caller.

Do not take a telephone call from a prospective employer at an inconvenient time. It is preferable to explain that you are about to leave for a meeting or are otherwise involved at the moment. You can ask to return the call at a specified time. If at all possible, the call should be returned the same day and as quickly as convenient for you and the caller. Return or accept the call at a time when you can sit down, concentrate on the content of the discussion, and remain undisturbed by extraneous noise or interruptions.

PREPARING FOR THE INITIAL CONTACT

For these phone calls, you must have your complete jobsearch file arranged in your notebook and readily available. It is imperative that you know what you wrote to the caller, and in the case of help wanted advertisements, in what points or areas of expertise the caller is most interested.

If the caller is responding to your mail marketing campaign, determine which of your letters was sent to him or her. You might ask several questions that will relate the caller's company to the appropriate letter. Then open your notebook to this letter and have it in front of you throughout the conversation. Be careful, however, not to allude to your having sent letters to more than a small number of firms.

If the call is in response to a blind advertisement, tell the caller you answered several such help wanted ads and ask to which he or she is referring. If the ad specified the company name, this single piece of information will help you find the letter.

The calls you receive will be of three types. The first is a simple request for an interview. The second is a request for additional information. The third is a conversation that can range from several questions to a nearly complete job interview by telephone.

It is easy to respond to the first two types of calls. If a company asks you to come for an interview, simply arrange a convenient time. If the interview requires travel, you can assume the expenses will be paid by the company. Unless the caller says something that leaves doubt in your mind, it is neither necessary nor advisable to ask. If the caller, for instance, expresses a wish to see you when you are in the area, you should expect to pay for the trip yourself. If you do not plan a trip that would make that interview convenient, explain this to the caller. State your interest in the company and ask if it would bring you to the city for an interview.

If the caller wishes additional information, it should be forwarded in a letter or cover letter with resume, as suggested in Chapter 10.

If the caller wants to discuss your background, respond to the questions. In doing so, however, remember that your objective is to secure a personal interview. For questions that might require an in-depth discussion, give a brief response and tell the caller you would like to discuss the matter in greater detail when you have an opportunity to meet him or her personally.

This can be a particularly effective method of not responding directly to questions concerning salary. Unless you are pressed by the caller to state a definite salary range or give your salary history, you can explain that your salary requirements will depend on a number of factors including the scope of the job, its future potential, and the cost of living in the particular city. Tell the caller that salary should not be a major problem but that you would prefer to discuss it after you have had an opportunity to visit the company and find out more about the position.

It is important that you take notes during the conversation. You should have a record of all questions asked by both you and the caller including a brief outline of the responses. This will give you a good indication of the items that are of major concern to the caller as well as the elements of your background and experience that are most attractive to him or her. You will then be able to elaborate on these points more effectively in a subsequent interview.

During the telephone conversation, be sure you get the complete name of the caller, spelled correctly, and his or her job title. For a difficult name, make a note of a phonetic spelling. This will assure your correct pronunciation later.

For each call you receive, start a file in the "Prospects" section of your notebook. Include a copy of your original letter, the notes from your telephone conversation, your confirming letter, and all subsequent notes and letters.

QUESTIONS TO EXPECT AND ASK

Review the sections "Questions to Expect" and "Questions to Ask" in Chapter 15. Depending on the scope and length of the telephone conversation, you may discuss several of these questions briefly or be asked to elaborate on some of the points in your letter. Be prepared to discuss your background and experience; explain the contribution you expect to make in your new position; and explain why you wish to make a change or why you left your last job.

Although the focus of this type of telephone call will be primarily on you and your background, you should also question the caller. Your questions should not match the scope or number you would ask in a personal interview. They should, however, enable you to adequately determine the primary concerns of the caller, as well as demonstrate some of your qualifications and increase the caller's interest in you. Ask about the responsibilities of the job, the authority the jobholder would be granted, and the particular problems that need attention.

The caller wants to know if you are sufficiently qualified to warrant the time and expense required to bring you to the company for a personal interview. Your objective is to stimulate his or her interest and prepare yourself for the subsequent meeting. Do this by concentrating on aspects of the job that are most important to the caller and most relevant to the problems needing immediate attention. You can then relate your past accomplishments to these problems.

Do not be boastful or unctuous; stick to your accomplishments. These are self-explanatory facts. Do not be pretentious. The caller knows more about the company and its problems than you do. Never allude to the possibility of your being a panacea or that you could handle the position with unusual ease. Keep in mind that you can be eliminated for being overly qualified as well as for not having adequate qualifications.

Once again, do not ask questions concerning salary, benefits, working conditions, or your own personal goals. All these items should be discussed in a personal meeting after the interviewer has decided in favor of you for the position.

ARRANGING A PERSONAL INTERVIEW

If near the end of your telephone conversation the caller has not brought up the subject of a personal interview, you should do so. Explain that you would like to have an opportunity to meet him or her personally and perhaps meet other people in the company. If any portion of the physical facilities would fall under your responsibility, mention also that you would like to visit the plant or office and look over the production equipment and see the material or process flow.

Such questions relate to your evaluation of the current situation as well as the contribution you can make to the company. They are directed toward securing a personal interview but should also allude to benefits the caller might get from this interview. The caller needs to feel that the interview will facilitate evaluation of your ability and perhaps introduce new ideas. The caller should also be able to anticipate an interesting discussion.

If the caller does not wish to set up an interview until a later date, maintain the initiative for the required follow-up. If the caller expresses a wish to talk to other candidates first, ask if you might check back about an appropriate date. Then call at that time, and again request a meeting.

INITIATING THE CALL

If you have stated in your letter that you will call the recipient, do so on the appointed date. If that person is interested in you, the content of your call will be similar to that discussed earlier. If not, use the call to gain as much information as you can. Ask the recipient how he or she felt about your letter, its content, or its wording. Ask for the names of any other companies you might contact. Ask for an introduction to these or the name of the person you should call.

If you do not get a satisfactory response to your mail marketing campaign, choose five or six firms and call them. Determine if they received and remember the letters. Question them about your approach, other companies you might contact, or the current demand for people with your qualifications. If you can spark their interest, ask if you might meet with them.

Use each call to its maximum advantage. Gather information that will help you and always try to set up a face-to-face meeting.

CONFIRMATION AND FOLLOW-UP

Unless you have arranged for an interview within one week of the date of your telephone conversation, this initial call must be confirmed with a letter. If a date has been set, the letter need only confirm the date, time, and place of the meeting. It should briefly express your interest in the job and in meeting the caller and his or her associates.

If an interview date has not been set, the letter should again confirm your interest in the job and recite several of the points discussed that were of primary interest to the caller. Then include several of your accomplishments that relate to these points. End the letter with a note of appreciation for the caller's interest and state your intention to follow the matter up.

Even if the result of the telephone call has been negative, write a confirming letter. If you are not interested in the job, this will be a simple thank-you note. If you are interested but the company does not appear interested in you, the letter should restate your desire for the job and indicate that you would like to talk to the company again if it is unsuccessful in finding a more qualified candidate.

Look at the examples of these four types of letters (#50–#53).

When placing follow-up telephone calls, you may find that your contact is hard to reach. He or she may not return your calls or may be in meetings continually. Do not let this affect your determination or interest in the company. Too many busy executives, or those who think they are busy, simply do not return calls. Keep trying. Leave messages with your contact's secretary and remember that it is always to your advantage to have this person on your side. Make sure the secretary knows why you are calling, and chat with her or him when you have an appropriate opportunity.

If you cannot reach your contact after repeated calls, send a mailgram (see #54). But be careful not to let any anger or anxiety show through. The mailgram should be a polite statement of your desire to talk with the recipient by phone, explaining your inability to reach him or her. If appropriate, refer to your earlier correspondence.

CHAPTER 15

INITIAL PERSONAL
INTERVIEWS

The initial personal interview will largely determine whether you receive a job offer. In many cases this will be your only opportunity to sell yourself to the prospective employer. It may also be your only opportunity to gather sufficient information about the job, the company, and the people to properly evaluate an offer.

You must be prepared for the interview. This will include doing research and recording pertinent facts about the company. You will prepare questions to ask and review questions that might be asked of you. You will also prepare yourself to manage and structure the interview to your own advantage.

If you have been invited to a company for an interview, it is because your earlier correspondence created an interest in you. Your first meeting will be your best opportunity to reinforce this interest and turn it into a job offer.

OBJECTIVES FOR YOU AND THE COMPANY

Your first and primary objective in a job interview is to convince the prospective employer that you can make a contribution to the organization, and that the company's investment in your salary and the time required to train you will produce a positive return.

This alone is not enough, however. In many cases you will be in competition with other individuals for the same position. You must then convince the employer that you are the best candidate or that your contributions would surpass those of other candidates.

You must also show the employer that you will be a compatible member of the organization. A company has character traits just as an individual does. These are formed from the predominant attitudes, lifestyles, and interrelationships of its employees, particularly those in its highest management. A company, for instance, may have a highly aggressive, extremely hard working president who has attracted an aggressive group of employees. Over a period of time the company itself begins to take on these character traits. A more conservative man or woman with an active family life would quickly feel ill at ease in this organization.

It is of equal importance that you gather sufficient information about the company and its members to evaluate the job in relation to your own qualifications, character, and objectives. Even though you may be able to sell yourself to a prospective employer, if you are not convinced that your contribution will exceed the company's investment in you, you would be ill advised to accept an offered position. Not only would you become frustrated by your lack of success, but you might also find your employment to be of short duration. The identical problem exists if you are incompatible with your colleagues or the potential of the job is not consistent with your career goals.

The primary objective of the company in an initial interview is an in-depth evaluation of you. It is as interested in your ability to contribute and your compatibility with its group as you are in selling yourself. It also wants to sell you on the company and the job. If it makes you an offer, it wants you to accept it.

Thus both you and the company are selling and evaluating. This similarity of objectives should facilitate discussion in the interview. Realizing that neither your objectives nor those of the company place you in an adversary position should put you at ease. Use this similarity of purpose to strive for the maximum exchange of information. This likely will result in a smooth and pleasant interview, and you will sell yourself without an obvious attempt to do so.

DRESS AND PERSONAL APPEARANCE

Regardless of what might be appropriate for wearing on the job you seek, go to an interview dressed conservatively. You will never be faulted if your dress is somewhat more formal than that of the person interviewing you. You will, however, find yourself out of place if you are not dressed at least to the interviewer's standard.

If you are a man, do not wear shirts, ties, or sports coats with loud colors or prints. Your hair should be neat and well groomed. If you normally wear your hair long or have had a beard for a substantial period of time, do not change your appearance for a job interview. Make certain all other aspects of your personal appearance and grooming are neat and appropriate. Cut and clean your fingernails. Do not wear rumpled or soiled clothing. Have your shoes polished. Do not wear white socks.

All the above comments for men should be translated into the appropriate style and grooming for women. In particular, women should not wear overly bright colors. Their nails should not be excessively long. Nail polish, if used at all, should be a muted color. Wear a minimum of jewelry. Shoes should be of moderate heel height that does not make you appear awkward or ill at ease. Do not dress provocatively or appear overly sexy. Although this might attract some men, in a job interview it will be for the wrong reason. As with men, women should not drastically change their appearance for a job interview.

Maintain good posture in your interview without appearing stiff. Look up; look the interviewer in the eye as you speak or are spoken to. This will contribute to both your appearance and self-confidence. Do not chew gum, bite your fingernails, or adopt other mannerisms that make you appear nervous or ill at ease. If you wish to smoke, first ask if it will disturb others in the room. Do not even ask, if there are no ash trays or smoking materials in sight.

WHAT TO TAKE WITH YOU

For all job interviews take an 8½"-by-11" note pad or clipboard, several copies of your resume, a written list of questions you expect to ask, and an outline of the information you have gathered about the company. This should include all your past correspondence concerning the job.

Do not take your jobsearch notebook or information or material you have prepared for other interviews. If your schedule necessitates your taking this material with you, leave it with your coat or in a briefcase in the reception area. You should appear well organized and prepared. Do not place yourself in a position that would cause you to fumble through numerous materials to locate information you need.

WHAT TO EXPECT

Most job interviews will be similar to any other business where the objective is an exchange of information. If you have followed the jobsearch manual procedures thoroughly, you will have a number of these interviews during the next few weeks. For this reason no single interview will be crucial to the success of your campaign. More than anything else, this should help put you at ease. You will have your best interviews when you are not quite convinced you would accept the position even if it should be offered. In this kind of atmosphere you will be genuinely interested in evaluating the company as well as selling yourself.

In most interviews you will meet with one or two members of the company. Sometimes additional people will be asked to join the meeting. If you feel outnumbered, diffuse this impression by commenting on your minority position, saying you do not want to be overpowered by their questions. They should understand that you also have questions to ask that are as important as theirs.

On rare occasions an interviewer may try to embarrass you or otherwise force you into a compromising position. Do not fall victim to this ploy. Simply use this information in your evaluation of the company and maintain your composure. If an interviewer persists in being offensive to such an extent that you would refuse an offer of employment, politely terminate the interview and leave.

The person facing you may know less about interview techniques than you. In addition, he or she may not be so well prepared. Use this to your advantage to put yourself and the interviewer at ease.

Be punctual, but do not wait over 45 minutes to be seen unless you had to travel a long distance for the meeting. After you have waited this long, explain that you have another appointment and ask if you can reschedule the interview at a more convenient time.

Do not start the interview with an extraneous comment about something in the room or an unrelated subject. Introduce yourself. If you start the conversation, do so with an expression of your interest in the job or company. Your research will have uncovered facts about the firm that can be used to substantiate this. Because the interviewer is also interested in the job and the company, the meeting will then flow smoothly.

You may be asked to have lunch with one or more members of the company. If you have the time, accept graciously. The luncheon conversation will usually be more general than that in a formal interview. This will give you an opportunity to assess the people with whom you might be working. Order a drink only if others at the table do so; then limit yourself to one. When ordering food, follow the example of your host in quantity and price. Do not start eating until everyone is served, and maintain good manners; you are still being judged.

Finally, expect to be rejected. Every interview will not result in a job offer. Do not let rejection affect your self-confidence or determination. You will have other opportunities.

RESEARCH PRIOR TO AN INTERVIEW

Prior to a job interview, gather pertinent information about the company and, if possible, about the person with whom you will talk. This information should be recorded in outline form and taken to the interview. If the company is a large national firm, go to the library and look it up in the Dun & Bradstreet or other appropriate directories. Consult *Who's Who in Finance and Industry* for the names of the people you might meet, and check for recent magazine articles concerning the company. The information you need is similar to, though not as complete as, that described in Chapter 13, "Special Situations." Review this part of the manual.

If you and any of the people you will meet have a mutual acquaintance, speak with this third party. Explain that you are going on a job interview and would like background information. There is little need to fear that your inquiry will be reported to the company. Most people will guard such requests in confidence. Even if they do not, this knowledge will only emphasize your thorough approach and, in most cases, will be viewed as appropriate. Do not, however, ask questions of a personal nature or those that might be resented if repeated to your interviewer.

As minimum information about the company, you should know its gross annual sales and total number of employees, as well as its major products and services. You should have information about its profitability and financial strength and a record of its growth over the past several years. Be conversant with its history and specific aspects of its performance in the area of your expertise.

MANAGING THE INTERVIEW

You can and should manage a job interview. This does not mean you should take charge, initiate all discussions, or overpower the interviewer. Simply guide the questions and discussion in a manner consistent with your objectives as well as those of the company.

In a job interview it is to your advantage to be on an equal status with the interviewer. If you do nothing except sit and respond to all questions asked, you will automatically be the interviewer's subordinate. This is the nature of a relationship between superior and subordinate. The superior asks questions; the subordinate answers. If, however, you ask enough questions to keep the interviewer talking at least half the time, you will be his or her equal.

This means you must be prepared, have reviewed questions that might be asked of you, and come to the interview with a list of questions you expect to ask. You must be alert and sensitive to the reactions and feelings of the interviewer. Do not persist with questions the interviewer cannot readily answer or dwell on subjects that are obviously uncomfortable for him or her. Guide the discussion into areas where you can use descriptions of your past accomplishments to reinforce your case. Although you should not introduce numerous extraneous subjects, it is wise to break a lengthy interview with a discussion of items that do not require continual concentration or mental effort.

Introduce any negative information about yourself or your background in such a way that it will do you the least harm or can be most easily explained. For instance, if you have a bad credit rating because of your own company's failure, ask about the financial strength of the interviewer's company. Explain that your interest is based on personal experience with your own undercapitalized firm that failed, and that this affected your credit. If you have held too many jobs, explain that you are asking a large number of questions to avoid making another mistake. Stress that you are looking for a career position, and describe your approach to the job market.

If there is a possibility of negative information becoming known to the interviewer, it is best to bring it up yourself. Show that you are not ashamed and that you have your future under control. Indicate that any negative aspects of your background are behind you and will not affect your contribution to a new company.

Most people speak approximately 150 words per minute. You can think at a far more rapid rate. Do not use this free time to allow your mind to wander as the interviewer presents questions or continues the discussion. Concentrate on the subject at hand. Pause if you wish to think before responding to a particularly difficult question. Use your mind's free time to consider the direction of the conversation. Then guide it with your responses and questions.

Over the past decade, role playing has become a widely used technique for training salespeople and others who are exposed to interview situations. At JOBSEARCH we gave all our clients a mock interview using these techniques. Everything from the introduction to the conclusion was kept as close as possible to a true job interview. We were as frequently surprised by clients who did well as by those who needed substantial coaching. In all cases, these interviews helped in structuring content as well as presentation.

If you have a close business friend who will take the time to give you a complete interview on a pro forma basis, this exercise can also help you prepare for job interviews. To do this effectively, define for your friend the position to be discussed and the type of company with which you might have an interview. Ask your friend to prepare his or her questions in advance. Then prepare yourself as thoroughly for this interview as for any other. At the appointed time, go to your friend and conduct yourself exactly as you would in a job interview. Continue the session to its logical conclusion before any comments or criticisms concerning your performance are made. When you have finished, your friend should give you his or her suggestions and criticisms on a completely frank basis.

QUESTIONS TO EXPECT

Most of the questions you will be asked in a job interview will concern your past career and its relation to the job being discussed. You will also be asked questions about yourself, your personal background, your likes and dislikes, and your motivation. On occasion you may consider a question too personal or inappropriate to the interview. If so, state your feeling about this and tactfully avoid responding.

Some portion of every job candidate's background requires explanation. This is one of the purposes of a job interview. When offering a required explanation, do not show any embarrassment or undue defensiveness about your past record. If you believe you are qualified to perform the job, concentrate on the factors that demonstrate these qualifications. When negative matters are introduced, explain how they do not relate to the job in question or how the lessons learned better equip you for your future career.

An accomplished interviewer will ask questions that are open-ended, that cannot be answered with a simple "yes" or "no" or with a short statement. Rather than asking what you liked about your last job, the interviewer will say, "Tell me about the aspects of your past job that you particularly enjoyed." Be ready to field these inquiries with a short description or discussion, but be sensitive to its length. Do not dwell on any subject that does not seem to interest the interviewer. Be ready to ask a question of your own to guide the conversation into another area.

The list of general questions (#55) in the workbook that might be asked in a job interview will be useful. Review all the questions and think about the responses you might offer. You should add to the list, in the spaces provided, 15 or 20 questions that relate specifically to your background or to the jobs for which you might interview.

Regardless of the questions asked, tell the truth. Elaborate only when it is to your advantage to do so, but then do not be repetitious. Answer all questions directly, and maintain a mutual exchange of information throughout.

QUESTIONS TO ASK

The questions you ask in an interview are frequently more important than your answers to those asked of you. You can show a person more about what you know and the contributions you can make to the organization by asking the right questions than by answering his or hers. Your questions can also guide the discussion into areas where you can appropriately comment on your past accomplishments to maximum advantage. Finally, by asking questions you will get the information you need to evaluate the company and the job.

Prepare your questions in advance of each interview. Write them legibly or type them, leaving spaces to enter the responses. The questions should be taken to the interview on your clipboard or note pad. As you receive answers, write a quick outline or several key words that will help you recall the response later. Although taking notes is unusual in a job interview, it is not impolite. Doing so should impress the interviewer with your thorough and organized approach. This will also reinforce the impression that you are there to evaluate the company and the job as well as sell yourself.

Your questions should be asked throughout the interview. They should be interspersed at appropriate points among questions from the interviewer. Do not divide the meeting into two distinct periods, one for the interviewer's questions and the other for yours. Instead you must maintain the atmosphere of an exchange of information.

The questions you ask should all relate to the company and the performance of the job under discussion. They should be a preview of the types of questions you might ask during your first several days at work. They should also give you information that will help you sell yourself, write your confirming correspondence, and prepare for subsequent meetings.

Check the list of general questions appropriate in any job interview (#56). In addition to queries of this type, you should ask those that relate only to the particular company or job. Your complete list should contain approximately 20 questions. Some of these will be answered in the course of the interview and therefore need not be asked. But attempt to get answers to all the questions you prepared.

An interview record form (#57) is provided for your use during job interviews. It contains information you can fill in prior to the meeting as well as space for your questions. Make a copy of this form for each interview. You will find it to be a convenient method of organizing your information.

When going on a job interview, try to arrive in the area 30 to 45 minutes early. Go to a nearby restaurant, order a cup of coffee (or your preferred nonalcoholic beverage), and read the list of questions you expect to be asked, the list of questions you anticipate asking, and your accomplishments list. Think about each of these. You will then be ready for the interview.

SUBJECTS TO AVOID

The above emphasis on questions and answers does not mean that portions of the interview should not be composed of general discussion. Some of this will not be related to you, the company, or the job. For instance, you may find that you and the interviewer have a common interest. It will be both pleasant and productive to briefly discuss this subject. Do not, however, devote too much time to these unrelated subjects. Keep the main discussion directed toward the primary purpose of the interview and be sure that you have time to adequately sell yourself and ask the questions you prepared. It is also advisable to avoid some subjects entirely. Politics, religion, and other topics often considered controversial are not appropriate for a job interview.

Early in a job interview, you will usually be questioned about your salary requirements. As in telephone interviews, this subject should be politely avoided until you are actually negotiating your salary and benefits package. In a meeting you might elaborate somewhat more than in a telephone conversation. Explain that salary is important to you—that you must work in order to gain your livelihood. Tell the interviewer, however, that it is not the only factor—and in some cases it may not even be the most important factor—on which you will base your decision. You can explain that you have a range of salary in mind, and are sure that the company has also considered a possible range. Say that when you know the company better and have received answers to a number of questions you wish to ask, you would hope that a mutual interest would be established. At this point both the company's and your salary range will probably have narrowed, and a discussion of salary would then be more productive. With a response of this type, you will usually not be pressed further. If you are, state a range that you consider reasonable and that you would accept.

In most job interviews you will meet the interviewer before he or she has seen a copy of your resume. In such cases, the interviewer may request one at the beginning of the interview. As previously explained in Chapter 9, you should tell the interviewer that you have prepared a resume, but tactfully suggest that you would prefer to leave it at the conclusion of your discussion.

PEOPLE TO MEET AND TOUR OF THE FACILITIES

If an initial job interview has been positive, it is appropriate for you to ask to meet other members of the firm. These would include persons in superior positions or in a position at the level of the job under discussion. Such meetings should be short. You will be introduced by the person who interviewed you. Briefly state that you are impressed by the company and are interested in the possibility of joining it. Any initiation of further discussion should be left to the other party. It may vary from a short, polite exchange to a summary of your entire interview. In any case, carefully judge the time these people have available for you. Do not continue the discussion if they seem pressed or occupied with other business.

Usually it is inappropriate for you to request to meet people who would be under your direct supervision in the new job. This can produce awkward situations as they try to prejudge their potential new boss. In some instances, they might not be cognizant of the changes that will bring you to the company. Also, remember that you might not be the candidate finally selected. In this instance, meeting subordinates would be premature.

If your new job would make you responsible for any portion of the facilities, you might request to tour them after the interview. Exceptions would be instances where plant facilities are prohibitively distant from the location of the interview, where a secret process or proprietary equipment is used, or where visitors to the plant are not permitted for reasons of safety or cleanliness. Make the suggestion only if the interviewer seems to have the time and if you feel the tour would be appropriate. If your interest in the facility is not genuine, do not ask. You may damage the impression left by the interview.

EXPENSE REIMBURSEMENT

At the conclusion of an interview that has required you to travel, ask if you should use the company's expense report form to request reimbursement. If this is not necessary, purchase a standard form at an office supply company or use a copy of form #5 in the workbook. When completing these expense records, be sure to enclose all appropriate receipts. In any case, do not send loose receipts with no recorded and totaled summary of expenses. This small detail is one more reflection of your businesslike approach to the job market and your sense of personal organization.

EMPLOYMENT APPLICATIONS

Many companies require the completion of employment applications regardless of the position. Because most hiring is done for lower-level personnel, these forms request information irrelevant to the job you seek. If the form is sent to you prior to an interview, complete and mail it or take it with you to the meeting. It should then, however, be treated like a resume and, if possible, not be given to the interviewer until the end of your discussion.

Avoid completing application forms in the company's office. Ask that you be allowed to do it at home after the interview, and state that you will mail it back to the company. It should then be completed with the same care afforded a resume. Where work experience is requested, it should be accomplishments oriented. Although the applications must be filled in completely, avoid giving negative information if possible.

A good practice with applications is to make a photocopy. Fill in the copy by hand and then use a typewriter to fill in the original. This will prevent messy erasures and improve the appearance of the completed application. If it is to be returned to the company by mail, do so promptly with a covering letter that can also serve the purpose of confirming the interview.

PSYCHOLOGICAL INTERVIEW AND TESTING

Some companies may request that you undergo a psychological interview or test as part of their hiring and evaluation procedure. Do not attempt to avoid such tests or interviews, but look on them as potentially helpful to both you and the company. This is an additional effort by the company to ensure that it makes the best possible decision in hiring key personnel. This kind of testing can also prevent you from making the mistake of joining an incompatible group or perhaps undertaking a job for which you are not suited.

After the tests are completed, it is appropriate that you request copies of any reports or test results. You might also ask to discuss the results with the psychologist even if you are not offered the position. These reports or discussions can be both interesting and enlightening. They can give you clues that are applicable to your career goals. If you are not offered the job, they can also help you direct the remainder of your jobsearch campaign.

An interview with an industrial psychologist will usually occur during a two- to three-hour meeting. The atmosphere will be cordial. The discussion will center on your past work experience and your family life with emphasis on your likes, dislikes, and motivations. This meeting is different from the job interview; you should not be trying to sell yourself directly nor should you be trying to impress the interviewer. Your objective is to state as frankly and thoroughly as possible who you are and why you are that way. In doing this, however, you will find it wise to again concentrate some portion of the discussion on your accomplishments. Use those that show your imagination, ability to work under pressure, or other personality traits. The psychologist will not try to judge your technical capabilities, but is rather primarily interested in you as a person.

Although you should ask fewer questions than you would in a job interview, the industrial psychologist can usually provide insight into the personalities and motivation of the individuals who make up the company's management. You may question the psychologist about this and let him or her know you are as interested as the company in finding associates with whom you fit.

There are two basic forms of psychological tests. The first requires answers to questions. Usually of the multiple choice type, these can be graded right or wrong. The second form asks you to describe yourself either with written phrases or by checking or ranking descriptive words. Make every effort to tell the truth when taking these tests. Do not try to second-guess the intent of the test or to create an overly favorable impression. The tests have been developed over a number of years and given to thousands of job applicants. Because they contain questions that will indicate your sincerity, you will do yourself a disservice by not being frank.

Hundreds of different tests exist to measure virtually all items of personality and intellect. They can be roughly divided into five types.

1. *Tests that measure ability.* These can be used to judge both intelligence and academic skills. At best, they predict readiness for academic work. They do not, however, measure either drive or determination, both of which have an influence on the ability of a person to perform an assigned task.

2. *Tests that measure temperament.* These tests define character traits such as aggressiveness, sociability, passivity versus activity, and dominance versus submissiveness.

3. *Tests that measure personal values.* These tests indicate an individual's likes and dislikes. They can also measure personal values such as honesty, loyalty, empathy, and desire for recognition. Both the temperament and the personal value tests can be used to determine suitable directions for job choices. They also give an indication of compatibility with a job and with another group of individuals.

4. *Interest areas.* These tests offer some measure of vocational interest as well as basic interest areas in the individual's life. Several commonly used tests measure the relative interest of an individual in working with his or her hands, with money, on artistic endeavors, in social services, at investigative tasks, and at administrative or conventional office tasks. One of these tests

correlates the likes and dislikes of an individual with those of a large number of people who have been successful in specific fields. This can give an indication of motivation, probable success, and compatibility in a chosen area of work.

5. *Mechanical aptitude.* These tests measure such items as the recognition of spatial relations, the understanding of things, and the ability to work with one's hands.

None of the above tests should place you under undue strain or pressure. They are easy and in many cases enjoyable to take. Approach them with a sense of interest and curiosity. They will serve both you and the potential employer well.

CONFIRMATION AND FOLLOW-UP

Every job interview, whether positive or not, must be confirmed within three days by letter. If you have not received a definite offer, use the notes from your interview to pick out several of the major problems of concern to your contact. Repeat these in your letter along with corresponding accomplishments. If you have received an offer, express your appreciation and interest, confirm the offer, and then state when you will respond.

For all pending prospects, your letter must conclude with a statement of the expected follow-up. If it can be done tactfully, maintain the initiative or indicate that you will phone if you have not heard from the company by a certain date.

Even in cases where you have been turned down, make every effort to leave the door open for future discussions. There may be a change in the company or in your jobsearch that would create a renewed interest.

Examples of these three types of letters are provided (#58–#60).

After each interview, add the notes and your confirming letter to the "Prospects" file in that section of your notebook. The follow-up should be put on your "To Do" list.

CHAPTER 16

SUBSEQUENT INTERVIEWS

If a company asks you to return for a second interview, it either plans to offer you the job or has narrowed its choices to you and one or two other candidates. If they have not been discussed earlier, this will be an appropriate time for negotiating salary and benefits. That will also afford both you and the company additional opportunity for evaluation and for exchanging more information.

For the male candidate, your wife may also be invited on the trip and to the interview or a dinner meeting. If a move is part of the new job, this will give her a chance to see the city and do preliminary house hunting. Many executives want to meet the wives of key employees prior to offering them a job. Make every effort to have her accompany you if she is invited. The cost of child care—should this be necessary while you are gone—will be a reimbursable expense and should not be difficult to arrange.

For the female candidate, being joined by your husband on a second interview has become increasingly prevalent. Many husbands are following as their wives move up the corporate ladder. Just as with the house-hunting trip, an appearance by the husband gives him an opportunity to evaluate job possibilities for himself in the new city and to begin gathering his own job-search information.

In only one instance did a JOBSEARCH client have to go on more than three interviews prior to receiving a job offer. In that particular case the man was called back seven times, gradually working his way up the corporate hierarchy from the hiring division to the headquarters office. It all took three months and substantial stamina. Two other candidates got discouraged and dropped out, but he finally received an offer that he accepted.

ADDITIONAL RESEARCH

From the information gathered in your initial interview, you should be able to judge the probable scope and content of subsequent meetings. This is a time to do additional research. If specific problems were explored in your first meeting and you believe they will be subjects of future discussion, ask for information that might assist you in reviewing the questions and possible solutions.

Go to the library and check for books on subjects that might give you background information on the industry or aspects of the job that may be unfamiliar to you. Call friends or associates who have handled jobs similar to the one you discussed. Question them about their problems, solutions, and results.

Review your notes from the initial interview. Try to pick out areas where additional discussion will further establish your competence for the job. Develop more specific questions concerning these areas and note your accomplishments that best reflect them. Review, and if possible expand, your sources of information about the company. You might now make calls to competitors or others in the industry that were too time consuming or expensive earlier.

You are now ready to negotiate a job offer. Show that you were interested enough to do some work on your own. The company will be impressed that the time between interviews was not wasted.

MANAGING THE INTERVIEW

Once again, tactfully manage the interview to your own advantage. In meeting persons for the second time, you will find the atmosphere more relaxed and the exchange of information freer. Your questions can be more specific. You can delve into company problems that might not have been appropriate subjects for your first encounter.

Meet additional company officers and key personnel to whom you were not introduced originally. If you did not visit important company facilities because of location or other reasons, suggest such a visit when setting up your subsequent interviews.

Try to gauge the interest and commitment of the company to both you and the position. If a job offer is not forthcoming and you feel the company has adequate information to make a decision, review the status and schedule of your jobsearch with them. Reiterate your interest in the job and the company. Then set a time with the interviewer when you will need a decision. Remember this must be done tactfully. If you have no other offers immediately pending, do not force a decision.

CONFIRMATION AND FOLLOW-UP

Again, a confirming letter is required. It should, however, be friendlier in tone and shorter than previous letters. Vary the content sufficiently to prevent the appearance of a stereotyped approach. Unless a specific problem was discussed, it is not necessary to repeat your accomplishments. If you have received a job offer, confirm it and indicate when you will respond. If you expect a future offer, state that you look forward to receiving it. Be positive and direct. You have sold yourself and now must take the time to evaluate this and other opportunities. Look over the example of a short confirming letter (#61).

CHAPTER 17

SALARY AND BENEFITS NEGOTIATIONS

In any interview or sequence of job interviews there will be a specific time when it will be to your advantage to negotiate the salary and benefits package to be included in a job offer. The time for this is the point when the interviewer has decided to try to get you to join the company. You are no longer selling yourself; your services are being bought.

It is not difficult to determine when this point arrives. The interviewer will begin to talk about you as if you were already a member of the group. The pronoun "we" will begin to be used instead of "you." The interviewer will speak increasingly in the future rather than the present and past tense.

This is not, however, a signal for you to begin the discussion of salary. It is only an indication that you can approach the negotiations directly when appropriate. In most cases the subject will be introduced by the interviewer. If that does not happen and you need the information for your own evaluation, simply state that you are interested in the position and would like to discuss the salary and benefits package. An interviewer who has decided to hire you will be glad to talk about these matters.

SOURCE OF COMPARATIVE SALARY INFORMATION

Before you begin negotiating your salary and benefits package, you must not only have a feeling for what the company might pay but also have information on competitive prices for your talents and experience. Except for a career change, the first and most obvious source of salary information is the past record of your own earnings. What were you worth to your last employer, and what has been the size and frequency of pay increases during your career? In most cases you can expect an increase with a change of position. This may even be one of your primary reasons for seeking a new job. If you have a past record of success, coupled with a history of increases in responsibility, use this record in your negotiations for higher pay.

Another source of salary information comes from the company itself. If you have answered an advertisement, a salary or salary range may have been mentioned. In your initial meetings, the interviewer may have given you an indication of the salary. If you have a close contact or friend in the company, you can ask that person about salary levels. Even without knowing the salary range for the position you seek, your contact or friend can probably give you some idea of the benefits package offered by the company, and can also tell you whether the company pays higher or lower salaries than others in the industry or in the same geographical area.

Other companies with positions similar to the one you seek are also good sources of salary information. If you are being interviewed for a job as senior accountant or controller, call a firm of similar size and type and ask to speak to the treasurer or vice-president of finance. Introduce yourself; explain that you are negotiating a position with another firm and would like information on comparative salaries. Describe the job briefly and name the company with whom you are negotiating. Several calls of this type should prove fruitful. It is advisable, however, not to call companies having close contact with your target firm.

In addition to these direct sources of salary information, published data are available concerning pay scales in almost all positions and industries. One of the best sources of this information is trade associations. Many of these conduct salary surveys periodically and publish the information for salaries in low, medium, and high ranges by area of the country and by different company sizes. As an example, the American Society for Personnel Administration publishes a biannual survey of salaries paid to personnel directors. Available for 18 regions of the country, this information also includes length of experience, age, scope of responsibility, years in present position, and level of education. With telephone calls to several associations in your field, you can quickly determine if such information is available and subscribe to it.

Trade journals occasionally publish salary surveys. Call the editorial offices of journals in your field and ask if they make these studies. If they do, request the latest issue of the magazine in which the survey was reported.

An excellent source of comparative salary information is help wanted advertisements in newspapers. In your ad answering campaign you will have gathered a number of clippings from various newspapers listing salary along with job titles and responsibilities. You might also review advertisements you did not answer.

The directors of employment agencies are usually well informed about salary levels in their area and generally will be glad to discuss them with you. Calls made to several agencies can be useful and productive.

The American Management Associations also publishes a number of salary surveys. These are listed nationally and for five regions of the country. Although the entire survey for any group is too expensive for your needs, the AMA will give you data by telephone, (212) 586-8100, at no charge for any one position. Their surveys and the prices for them are:

Top Management	$300
Middle Management	250
Professional/Scientific	220
Supervisory Management	165
Sales Personnel	165
Technician	120
Office Personnel	120

The AMA information is particularly useful for comparative salaries at the highest levels of management. These are difficult to obtain from other sources.

In addition to your research on salaries, if your new job will require moving your family, you should review the relative cost of living in cities where you may receive an offer. Real estate agents in these cities are good sources of information concerning housing costs and can sometimes give you comparative cost-of-living data. A cost-of-living index by city is also available from the chamber of commerce and the U.S. Department of Labor, Bureau of Labor Statistics.

All the information you receive from these various sources must be interpreted with care. The salary the company is willing to pay and the salary you are willing to accept will depend on numerous items, the majority of which are intangible. Among these, you should take into consideration the following:

Living cost in the area
Current supply of your specific talents in the job market
Current demand for your talents
Size of the company
The industry in which the company participates
The type of company or organization
How well you have sold yourself for the position
The trade-off between salary and benefits
The financial strength of the company
The future potential for increased earnings
The trade-off between salary and potential equity
The company's ability to alter pay scales set by policy

From an evaluation of this information, you should be able to establish a realistic salary range equitable for both you and the company. Prior to the start of negotiations, write down this range together with the factors and data on which it is based.

THE NEGOTIATION

Just as you do, the company will also have a range of salary it considers equitable. Although it is not always possible, it is to your advantage for the person with whom you are negotiating to disclose the company's range or offering salary as an introduction to the negotiations. If this salary is not compatible with your expectations, state that it is close or a little lower than what you had in mind. Then proceed to a discussion of benefits. In most cases the company will pay at least slightly more than the initial salary offered. You should leave the door open to take advantage of this possibility.

If the offered salary is acceptable, say that it is consistent with or quite close to your objective. Do not indicate immediate acceptance of the first offer. After you have received other offers, you may want to ask for more.

If you are placed in the position of having to disclose your desired salary before knowing what the company will offer, do not give a range but state a definite figure at the high end of what you expect. If this is acceptable, it will immediately become the basis for your starting salary. If it does not appear to be acceptable, you can then discuss the reasons and the data that support your request. Indicate some flexibility and suggest that both you and the company consider the matter further. In any case, state that you are not in a position to accept an offer immediately as you have other possibilities to evaluate.

Regardless of whether your starting salary is definitely fixed during these conversations, do not accept the job until you have had time to properly evaluate all its aspects and to conclude negotiations with other interested companies.

If you have sold yourself well and the company would like to have you join the organization, do not let a salary discrepancy completely rupture negotiations. Even if the offered salary is substantially lower than what you want, indicate that you are interested in the position. Explain that the salary is lower than what you expect but that you would like to consider it for a few days or weeks. Request that the company review your qualifications and potential contribution in relation to the salary offered. Depending on other offers you receive, you may wish to accept the position at a lower salary than you expected or subsequently convince the company to increase the starting salary or include other benefits that might make it acceptable.

A JOBSEARCH client interviewing for a position as senior vice-president of operations for a bank holding company found every aspect of the job and offer acceptable except salary. The two parties were close to agreement but the salary offered was not quite what he wanted. He was, however, an unknown quantity for the bank since he had no prior banking experience. He used this point to his advantage by getting the bank to agree to a salary review after four months instead of one year. All he needed was a little time, he explained, to prove his value. Four months later he had the salary he wanted.

Salary negotiations should result in your getting all the information you need to evaluate the offer. You will then be in a position to call the company at a later date and say one of the following:

"I would like to accept the position offered."
"I will accept the position if we can agree on a starting salary of _____."
"I will accept the position if we can agree on a starting salary of _____ together with _____."

The completion of this last sentence might be an expanded benefits package, additional perquisites, or guaranteed salary review after a shorter than customary period of time.

In a salary negotiation, do not forget that a company's initial offer is just that—an offer. In most cases you can get the company to increase it. Although you cannot afford to appear unreasonable, you naturally want to be paid as much as you are worth to your new company. If it pays you less than this, you will be unhappy. If it pays you more, your new job may be one of short duration. The negotiation is used to arrive at the point that is equitable for both parties.

FRINGE BENEFITS AND PERQUISITES

An immense range of fringe benefits is offered by American business. Except at the highest levels of a company, the benefits package is not usually open to much negotiation. Nevertheless, you should discuss all benefits offered and gather sufficient data to evaluate the monetary equivalent of each.

If certain desired benefits are not offered, you can discuss them with the expectation of their being provided in your case or of your receiving a compensating salary increase. Because fringe benefits are offered equally to all employees at a certain level, companies usually have more latitude in setting salaries than benefits.

Following is a list of fringe benefits generally arranged in the order of most common to most rare with some indication of, or sources of information about, their monetary value.

Vacation and holidays. Although all companies offer both these items, policy and extent differ widely. In a job change you may find that you lose your vacation privileges until you have been on the job for a year. Be specific when discussing this question. Vacation policy for new employees is frequently flexible. If you have planned a summer vacation that is not consistent with company policy, mention this and see if the vacation waiting period might be modified in your case. Do not do this, however, if you would not have a minimum of four months on the job prior to your vacation. Convert your yearly salary to a daily rate by dividing by 250. Use this figure to determine the monetary value of vacations and holidays.

Group insurance package. Most companies offer a standard group insurance package to employees. These frequently provide different coverage for different groups. The most extensive coverage is offered to top executives. A different package is available for middle management and other salaried personnel. Insurance for hourly paid personnel either is determined by union contract or is again a separate plan. When discussing the company's program, be careful to determine whether it is a contributory program requiring that a portion of the premiums be paid by the employee or whether it is fully company-paid. In contributory programs, the employee portion is usually deducted directly from the salary at each pay period. Ask the exact amount of these deductions for each type of insurance offered. Also determine the extent of coverage for each type of insurance. With this information you can call a local insurance agent to check out the cost of similar coverage on an individual basis. In the order of frequency offered, these group plans will cover hospitalization, life, accident, major medical, disability, and dental expenses.

Sick leave and pay. As with vacation and holidays, determine the sick leave policy of the company including the number of days of salary continuation. If it is a standard number of days per year, convert these days into their salary value.

Automobile. This is a company benefit that can be of substantial monetary value to an employee. Depending on the amount of travel for both business and pleasure, the value to you of a company car will vary between $2,000 and $4,000 per year. For the employee this can be an attractive method of compensation. It represents a replacement for income on which no income taxes are paid. It is equally attractive to the company because its monetary value does not become part of the salary base for payroll taxes, pension benefits, and other fringes. A company car should be evaluated with care. It can frequently make an otherwise low salary both attractive and competitive.

Expense account and travel reimbursement. Ask about the expense account and travel reimbursement policy of the company. Except for the highest level of executives, these perquisites will generally include reimbursement only for expenses incurred on company business. Policies vary widely, however. Some companies pay a standard per diem for travel, room, and board that may not be adequate to cover your normal travel expenses. If this is the case and much travel is required, it will have the effect of a straight reduction in your pay.

Retirement and pension plans. Although you may be years away from retirement, these plans are still important to your job evaluation and future security. As with insurance programs, they are sometimes contributory. If this is the case, determine the amount that will be deducted from your salary. Also inquire about the company's contribution in your specific case. If you are young, it is of utmost importance that you ask about the vesting provisions of the plan. After you have served a certain number of years with the company, it provides for payment at retirement age of a portion of the benefits, even though you might leave prior to normal retirement.

Profit sharing and bonus. If these are offered, determine if they are paid yearly or become part of a deferred-earnings pension plan. They will work to your best advantage if they are cash payments calculated on the basis of an established formula. It is also preferable for you to be in a position to have direct influence over the portion of profits that is included in the formula. These plans are least attractive if they are based only on the discretion of a company management group of which you are not a member.

Stock options. In a small company this can be an excellent method of gaining future equity. In larger companies these options represent a form of deferred-earnings payments with favorable tax consequences. If stock options are a major portion of your benefits package, check with an accountant to determine the tax implications when the options are granted and exercised. The accountant can also estimate the monetary value of the options if it is not evident from the plan or company contribution.

Educational opportunity. Many companies will pay all or a portion of the cost of continuing education for their employees. If you intend to make use of this benefit, determine if your curriculum is consistent with the reimbursement policies of the company. This can be an attractive fringe benefit.

Sabbaticals. Some professional groups and companies offer periodic sabbaticals to technical or high-level management personnel for study or research. If you work in an area of rapidly changing technology, this can be indeed attractive. When sabbaticals are offered, ask if your salary or a portion of it will be continued while you are off.

Personal time off. Determine the policies of the corporation in allowing time off for necessary personal business, deaths in the family, or other items that might require your attention during regular business hours.

Country club memberships. These are generally offered only to the highest-level executives or to those who must entertain extensively in the local area. If such a perquisite is offered, ask about the choice of clubs and learn something about their membership and status. Call the club to ask what the dues are.

Medical payment plan. These plans pay all medical expenses for select groups of company executives and their families, including doctors' visits and prescription drugs. For a large family these plans can represent substantial monetary value. Review the medical deductions on your income tax forms for the past several years to determine their value to you.

Education for children. A few companies offer college scholarships for dependent children of their highest-level employees. Although this benefit is rare, the monetary value of such a plan is substantial.

MOVING EXPENSES

When a new job requires you to move, discuss moving reimbursement in detail. If you have received a job offer as a result of a response to a national help wanted advertisement, it is customary for the company to cover the moving expenses for your family. If, on the other hand, you search out your new company, it may not have assumed that it would incur these costs. This can be a major expense that might affect your willingness to accept a new position.

You must not only ascertain the extent of the moving cost to be reimbursed, but also determine the company policy concerning temporary living expenses while you are searching for a new home.

Of equal importance is the company's policy concerning the sale of your present residence. Most companies will not indemnify you for costs incurred in the sale of your home. Some will pick up mortgage payments if the sale entails a prolonged period of time. Some will pay the real estate commission on the sale. A few will actually buy your home at an appraised value, allow you to immediately purchase a new residence and begin your job with the least inconvenience.

There are also income tax considerations in moving-expense reimbursement. Some moving expenses are deductible for federal tax purposes, but these are limited to a maximum amount. If you are reimbursed for an amount exceeding this maximum, the excess may become taxable income. Ask an accountant about these expenses. If the company intends to indemnify you for all moving costs, try to have it include the estimated tax liability on reimbursements that are classed as income.

SALARY REVIEWS

As we have discussed earlier, salary reviews can also be important in your negotiations for a new position. At the very least, determine the company's policies on salary reviews including both cost-of-living adjustments and merit pay increases. If your negotiated salary is somewhat lower than you expected, you might compensate for this by having the company agree to a salary review after a short period. This would be before the normal review period but after you have had sufficient time to demonstrate your contribution. Four to six months is usually a reasonable period.

OPPORTUNITY FOR PROMOTION

This point should be discussed with care, particularly if your career objectives require a number of increases in job responsibilities or elevations of job status. You might briefly review your five- and ten-year objectives with your future superior. Discuss how you expect to reach these goals. Determine the past promotion practices of the company, the ages of your immediate superiors, and the ages of others in the company who have attained the levels you seek.

Do not give your future employer the impression that if you are not promoted after a brief period you will leave. On the other hand, unless you are only a few years from retirement, your employer should understand that you will not sit complacently in your new job for the rest of your career. The potential for advancement is an appropriate factor in all job evaluations.

EMPLOYMENT CONTRACTS AND TERMINATION AGREEMENTS

Employment contracts are normally given only to seasoned executives in high positions. Usually their purpose is to compensate an executive who leaves a stable job for one of higher exposure and risk. A younger person should be more willing to let job and future remuneration depend on his or her own capabilities and contributions. If you are in the latter situation, discuss employment contracts only if one is offered by the potential employer.

If an employment contract includes a "noncompete" agreement, consider it with care. This can prevent your working for a competitor or entering the same business as that of your employer for a specified number of years after you leave or are terminated. You may wish to have such a clause reviewed by a lawyer. Do not sign it perfunctorily. Years later it may cause problems for your career.

A friend of mine signed such an agreement in 1955. Twenty years later, at age 72, he wanted to do some consulting work on a new product development. The old agreement surfaced and ended his employment.

Termination agreements are sometimes included in employment contracts for jobs involving high professional risks. This might be a top executive position with an unprofitable or failing company or a management position that historically has been subject to high turnover. These agreements stipulate the termination provisions or severance benefits if the employee for any reason does not work out in the new position. Such agreements are appropriate but should be discussed only under rare circumstances.

CONFIRMATION BY LETTER

After you and the potential employer have reached agreement on all aspects of the offer, it should be confirmed in writing. If you think the potential employer might normally do this, ask whether you should confirm the offer or whether the company would prefer to do it. If you write the letter, again express your interest in the job and indicate a definite time by which you will respond. An example of such a letter appears in the workbook (#59).

TIMING FOR ACCEPTANCE

Depending on how far along you are in your jobsearch campaign and on additional offers you expect to receive, the time during which you can appropriately consider an offer will vary from a few days to a month. Except in rare circumstances, do not expect a potential employer to wait more than one month for your reply. In most cases you should limit this maximum time to three weeks. Your objective is to gain only sufficient time to expedite and evaluate additional offers. To do this, immediately advise other companies that showed an interest in you that you have an offer to which you must respond by the specified date. This tactic should not be used, however, unless you are definitely interested in the initial offer. If the other company is not ready to make a decision, it may turn you down prematurely.

RECORD OF OFFERS

Keep a record of each job offer by filling in form #62. For each offer, combine this record with all correspondence in your "Prospects" file. Then use this information in your evaluation of the jobs and your next career move.

CHAPTER 18

EVALUATION OF JOB OFFERS

After you have received all the job offers you expect, thoroughly evaluate each — both individually and in comparison with the others.

Even if you have received only one, it will be necessary to evaluate it and review all other responses from your search. This evaluation will concern three possible options: to accept the offer, to delay acceptance and recontact other companies that indicated a future interest, or to reject it and return to your jobsearch compaign with a new and expanded effort.

An evaluation form (#63) is provided in the workbook. It includes both concrete and abstract criteria for job evaluation. These relate to the job targets and career goals you established in Chapters 4 and 5 with additional items concerning the company and the job. Several blank spaces are provided for other criteria that might be of particular interest to you.

When using this form you may rank each item first, second, and third for different job offers. You may rank each item on a scale of one to ten individually. Or if you prefer, simply enter "good," "fair," or "poor." Some items will be more important to you than others.

In addition, your final job decision must include intuition as well as preference by rank. Because of this, do not total the columns and then choose a job based on the highest numerical score. Rather, consider each point carefully and then consider the total job. Your decision will establish the initial step for your entire future career.

RENEGOTIATION

After you have finished your first evaluation, you may find one job or company that you prefer but would reject for one specific reason — such as salary or scope of responsibility. In such a case, consider phoning your contact or making an appointment for a meeting at the company. Tell your contact why you prefer the company; then review the deficiencies in its offer. In the case of salary, you might ask if the company would match or perhaps come closer to that offered by another firm.

This form of renegotiation should not be used unless your preference and the competing offer are genuine. You must be prepared to disclose the name of the other firm as well as the specifics of its offer. If this renegotiation proves fruitful, be prepared to accept the new position immediately. If it is not successful, you will have compromised your position with the preferred company and will find it difficult not to accept the offer from the competing firm.

ADVISING THE OFFERING FIRMS

After you have accepted an offer and established a starting date for your new job, confirm this acceptance in writing. Refer to the earlier written confirmation of the offer, but repeat only the specifics that were later modified (see the sample letter, #64).

In addition, write to each of the other firms that made you an offer. This letter (sample #65) should politely thank the firm for its consideration and advise it that you have accepted a position elsewhere. The firm will then know it should consider other candidates or return to its own search to fill the position.

CHAPTER 19

THE MOVE

Ronald Marque needed to change careers in order to use his educational training. He went from a line job in mortgage banking to a senior staff financial analyst's position. William Naff started out looking for a controller's position; he is now a legal administrator for a law firm. Carter Harlen is executive director of a new natural history museum that needed his fund-raising ability combined with his business administration background. Other successful JOBSEARCH clients have been mentioned throughout this book. You can join them. It takes only good judgment, hard work, and perseverance.

My father was an executive with an international engineering/construction firm. When asked the secret of his success, he replied that it was a combination of luck and hard work. "But the strangest thing," he added, "is that the harder I work, the luckier I get."

With your successful jobsearch campaign now behind, you must prepare to take your new position. If you are currently employed, it will of course be necessary for you to resign. The starting date you establish for your new job should permit you sufficient time for an orderly completion or transfer of unfinished work with your old company. During this period, take care to maintain good relations with your former employer and to avoid adversely affecting the morale of your colleagues. Sometime in the future you may need the help of some of these people.

When you resign, do so politely but decisively. Do not try to bargain with your employer before resigning. If you use your offer as a tool to gain concessions in your current job, you may succeed but at the price of severely damaging your credibility and future chances for promotion. Your employer will know or may learn that the new job did not just come to you. It is likely that your employer will discover that you sought the new job with the intention of leaving your current one, and may expect you to do this again in the future.

Even if your current employer makes an unsolicited counteroffer, do not acquiesce. You have accepted employment with a new firm and must honor your commitment to it. If you wanted to stay with your current company, you should have had a frank discussion about your job and its conditions before you began your search.

RELATIONS WITH YOUR NEW EMPLOYER

Your new employer will be anxious to have you join the organization. You will also be excited about the change, the challenge, and the opportunity. If it seems appropriate, you might request preliminary information for study during the transition period. You might also meet on occasion with your new associates. You should not, however, act as though you are on the job until you are there on a full-time, salaried basis.

If your new employer is a long distance from where you now live or if you do not have occasion for contact during the transition period, do not show up on your starting date unannounced. Call several days in advance to remind the company that you will report for work at a specified time.

During the period of transition and your first few days on the new job, do not concentrate on insignificant matters that relate to your own comfort. Do not worry about your office, desk, or other facilities. Concentrate on learning about the job at hand and probing for the problems that need your initial attention. This is what you were hired to do.

Your new job was found by dint of a thorough and concerted effort. You have had an opportunity to investigate employment possibilities with a large number of companies. You have evaluated and accepted a job offer that should be consistent with your initial objectives. You must now give your new employer your best effort.

FINAL CORRESPONDENCE

Throughout your jobsearch campaign you received the advice and assistance of a large number of people. As a courtesy, write to each of them informing them of the results of your search and thanking them for their help. Follow the sample letter #66. Compile the mailing list for these letters by going through your entire jobsearch file. Write a short note to everyone who offered real assistance. At some future date, you might again need the help of these persons.

THE
JOBSEARCH
WORKBOOK

WORK SCHEDULE

NAME   DATE

Item	Scheduled Completion Date	Modified Completion Date	Actual Completion Date
Start date			
Order stationery and photographs			
Establish information sources			
Complete accomplishments list			
Establish career goals			
Define marketing targets			
Draft resume			
Check reference responses			
Type and copy resume			
Complete personal contacts list			
Draft help wanted reply letters			
Start answering help wanted ads			
Draft direct mail letters			
Complete direct mail address lists			
Autotype direct mail letters			
Send direct mail letters			
Complete personal contacts			
Complete other contacts			
Examine special situations			
Complete special situation information			
Contacts for special situations			
Complete job interviews			
Evaluate job offers			
Accept new job			
Report to work			

2

SUMMARY AND MISCELLANEOUS EXPENSE RECORD

NAME _____

Date	Item	Expense	Total
	Jobsearch Manual		

AUTOMOBILE EXPENSE RECORD

NAME _____

Date	Location	Person seen	Mileage	@17¢/Mile	Total

TELEPHONE EXPENSE RECORD

NAME _____

Date	City called	Person called	Toll Charges	Add 10% Tax & Service	Total	Date Paid

TRAVEL EXPENSE REPORT

Report No.:
Name: Date:

Date						
Itinerary from						
To or at: Item						Totals
Transportation — Personal car						
Airplane						
Rental car						
Limousine or rail						
Taxi						
Parking						
Lodging						
Meals — Breakfast						
Lunch						
Dinner						
Telephone						
Miscellaneous						
Total						
Purpose of trip						

Signature _____

H. LEE RUST
3404 EAST BRIARCLIFF ROAD
BIRMINGHAM, ALABAMA 35223
TELEPHONE (205) 967-9728

Mr. William F. Blakley, President   February 10, 1977
Southeastern Manufacturing, Inc.
2200 Fifth Avenue, North
Birmingham, Alabama 35202

Dear Mr. Blakley:

    I have a business associate and friend who, as controller for a
large food distributor, designed and implemented an inventory control
system which cut losses and credits by $2,500 weekly. Because you may
need a controller or financial executive with this kind of talent, you
may be interested in a few of his other accomplishments.

   --As treasurer or controller of four companies ranging in size from
     $500,000 to over $70 million in annual sales, he designed and
     implemented systems for converting all accounting functions to
     computer operations, including work with minicomputers, service
     bureaus, and large systems.
   --He recognized the need at a franchise operation and set up a buyers'
     guide showing inventory movement and source and delivery
     information. This allowed a 50% reduction in purchasing department
     personnel.
   --He designed installment sales accounting procedures including an
     automatic delinquency notice system which reduced average delinquent
     time on accounts receivable by 60%.
   --In cash control, he set up and managed an investment portfolio which
     increased after-tax profits on invested funds by $25,000 annually.

    Because this man is now employed with a company you probably know, I
must keep his name confidential until a mutual interest is established.
He has 20 years of corporate accounting and financial experience, has an
accounting degree from the University of Alabama, and has taken
continuing education courses in computer use, tax procedures, accounting,
and speed reading.
    If you would like to meet with this person or further discuss his
background and experience, please call me at the above number after 5:00
P.M. or during the weekend. I might add that this letter is personal. I
will not receive a commission or fee of any kind as a consequence of
employment that might result.

                                        Yours truly,

                                        H. Lee Rust

FINANCIAL
ACCOUNT
EXECUTIVE

New opportunity for person with good agency/financial experience. Someone with background in servicing and leading a sizable bank, in marketing, or in advertising operation would be ideal. Fine growth potential. Midwest. 4A agency. Profit sharing plan. Young full-service team. Need your resume and income range.

Box 267 AD COUNSEL JOURNAL
2764 Rush St., Atlanta, Ga. 47165

H. LEE RUST
3404 EAST BRIARCLIFF ROAD
BIRMINGHAM, ALABAMA 35223
TELEPHONE (205) 967-9728

February 10, 1977

Box 267
Ad Counsel Journal
2764 Rush Street
Atlanta, Georgia 47165

Dear Sir:

I have a business associate and friend who is a leader of an innovative marketing organization in a $1.2-billion bank holding company. He managed the 10th anniversary celebration of a major subsidiary that drew 25,000 people through ten branches in one day.

Because you advertised for a financial account executive, I thought you would be interested in some of his other accomplishments.

- —He led a task force which was used in special marketing problem situations for both the holding company and its bank subsidiaries.
- —He wrote print ads and brochure copy for a Campus Plan Account promotion which opened 2,000 new accounts in the first six months.
- —For a new, small-town bank, he created and directed the grand opening promotion that drew traffic equal to 10% of the town's population.
- —He personally sold bank services and solicited new accounts, exceeding his annual quota by over $60,000.

Because you probably know this man's current employer, I cannot disclose his name until a mutual interest is established. However, a marketing degree and four years with an in-house bank agency have prepared him to respond to the needs of your advertised position.

If you would like to meet with him or further discuss his background and experience, please call me at (205) 669-0711 or, after 5:00 P.M., at the above number. I might add that this letter is being written as a personal favor. I will not receive a commission or fee of any kind should you reach agreement on his employment.

Cordially,

H. Lee Rust

H. LEE RUST
3404 EAST BRIARCLIFF ROAD
BIRMINGHAM, ALABAMA 35223
TELEPHONE (205) 967-9728

BUSINESS REFERENCE BOOKS
AVAILABLE AT PUBLIC LIBRARIES

Million Dollar Directory
Middle Market Directory
Metalworking Directory
Principal International Business
　　　Dun & Bradstreet
　　　99 Church Street
　　　New York, New York　10007

Businesses are listed alphabetically, geographically, and by Standard Industrial Classification (SIC) code. Names of company officers are also shown.

Standard Industrial Classification Code Manual
　　　Superintendent of Documents
　　　U.S. Government Printing Office
　　　Washington, D.C.　20402

Ulrich's International Periodicals Directory
　　　R. R. Bowker Company
　　　1180 Avenue of the Americas
　　　New York, New York　10036

Encyclopedia of Business Information Sources
　　　Gale Research Company
　　　Book Tower
　　　Detroit, Michigan　48226

Lists source books, periodicals, organizations, directories, handbooks, and bibliographies by category, topic, and geographical location.

Encyclopedia of Associations
　　　Gale Research Company
　　　Book Tower
　　　Detroit, Michigan　48226

Listing by key words.

Directory of European Associations
　　　Gale Research Company
　　　Book Tower
　　　Detroit, Michigan　48226

Listing by category number.

Guide to American Directories
   B. Klein Publications, Inc.
   Coral Springs, Florida 33134
   Rye, New York   10580

Listing of specialized directories and other information sources.

Thomas Register of American Manufacturers
   Thomas Publishing Company
   One Penn Plaza
   New York, New York   10001

Company listing by products manufacturer; no names of individuals.

E/MJ Directory of Mining and Metal Processing Operations
Consultants and Consulting Organizations Directory
Pharmaceutical and Cosmetics Firms, U.S.A.
Worldwide Directory of Computer Companies
Directory of Foreign Manufacturers in the United States

Special trade directories.

Franchise Opportunities Handbook
   U.S. Department of Commerce
   Superintendent of Documents
   U.S. Government Printing Office
   Washington, D.C.   20402

Index by category.

Who's Who in Finance and Industry
   Marquis' Who's Who, Inc.
   200 East Chicago Street
   Chicago, Illinois 60611

Listing by individual's name and company names, including titles and biographical data for over 20,000 American business leaders.

Business Periodicals Index
   The H. W. Wilson Company
   950 University Avenue
   Bronx, New York 10452

This is a subject index to articles that have appeared in over a hundred business magazines. It is published monthly and is usually available as far back as ten years.

PERSONAL NET WORTH

NAME: _____   DATE: _____

ASSETS

Cash on hand and in bank   _____

Savings account balance   _____

Accounts receivable   _____

Notes receivable   _____

Stocks and bonds, readily salable   _____

Stocks and bonds, closely held   _____

Cash value of life insurance   _____

Real estate owned, home   _____

Real estate owned, other   _____

Automobiles owned   _____

Personal property, household furnishings _____

Personal property, jewelry, silver, art _____

Personal property, other   _____

Other assets   _____

                          Total Assets   _____

LIABILITIES

Bills on hand   _____

Notes payable to banks   _____

Notes payable to others   _____

Real estate mortgage, home   _____

Real estate mortgage, other   _____

Auto loan balance   _____

Installment purchase loan balances   _____

Other debts   _____

                     Total Liabilities   _____

                          Net Worth   _____

      Total Liabilities and Net Worth   _____

MONTHLY CASH FLOW PROJECTION

NAME _____   DATE _____

Beginning cash balance   _____   _____   _____   _____

   Income   _____   _____   _____   _____

   Disbursements   _____   _____   _____   _____

Ending cash balance   _____   _____   _____   _____

	MONTH 1	2	3	4
Salary	_____	_____	_____	_____
Severance benefits	_____	_____	_____	_____
Other company payments	_____	_____	_____	_____
Retirement income interest	_____	_____	_____	_____
Unemployment compensation	_____	_____	_____	_____
Spouse's income	_____	_____	_____	_____
Dividends	_____	_____	_____	_____
Rental income	_____	_____	_____	_____
Tax refund	_____	_____	_____	_____
Cash from savings	_____	_____	_____	_____
Cash from loans	_____	_____	_____	_____
Cash from life insurance	_____	_____	_____	_____
Repayment of debts owed me	_____	_____	_____	_____
Other income	_____	_____	_____	_____
_____	_____	_____	_____	_____
Total income	_____	_____	_____	_____

MONTHLY CASH FLOW PROJECTION
Disbursements

NAME _____   DATE _____

	MONTH 1	2	3	4
Bills on hand				
Mortgages				
Auto loan payments				
Installment loan payments				
Utilities				
Telephone				
Automobile expense				
Insurance premiums				
Food				
Clothing				
Drugs and medical				
Household items				
Personal items				
Laundry and dry cleaning				
Dues and subscriptions				
Taxes				
Gifts				
Education				
Child care or domestic services				
Recreation and entertainment				
Miscellaneous				
Jobsearch expense				
Total disbursements				

JOBSEARCH EXPENSE ESTIMATE

NAME _____   DATE _____

Personal stationery   _____

Resume photographs   _____

Subscriptions   _____

Reference books   _____

Other information   _____

Secretarial services   _____

Copying expense   _____

Long—distance telephone calls   _____

Local travel and parking   _____

Other travel   _____

Autotyping services   _____

Postage   _____

Other expenses   _____

_____   _____

_____   _____

_____   _____

                         Total expenses   _____

DIRECT JOB—RELATED ACCOMPLISHMENTS

NAME _____   DATE _____

Title, Company Name, City, and State

_____ 1. _____
Period in years
_____

2. _____

_____

3. _____

_____

4. _____

_____

5. _____

_____

_____ 1. _____

_____

2. _____

_____

3. _____

_____

4. _____

_____

5. _____

_____

13

DIRECT JOB-RELATED ACCOMPLISHMENTS

NAME _____   DATE _____

Title, Company Name, City, and State

_____ 1. _____

Period in years

_____

2. _____

_____

3. _____

_____

4. _____

_____

5. _____

_____

_____ 1. _____

_____

2. _____

_____

3. _____

_____

4. _____

_____

5. _____

_____

13

DIRECT JOB—RELATED ACCOMPLISHMENTS

NAME _____   DATE _____

Title, Company Name, City, and State

_____ 1. _____
Period in years
_____

2. _____
_____

3. _____
_____

4. _____
_____

5. _____
_____

_____ 1. _____
_____

2. _____
_____

3. _____
_____

4. _____
_____

5. _____
_____

14

INDIRECT JOB-RELATED ACCOMPLISHMENTS

NAME _____   DATE _____

Title, Company Name, City, and State

_____ 1. _____
   Period in years

2. _____

3. _____

_____ 1. _____

2. _____

3. _____

_____ 1. _____

2. _____

3. _____

EDUCATIONAL ACCOMPLISHMENTS

NAME _____   DATE _____

Degree Received, Institution, City, and State

_____ 1. _____

Period in years

_____

2. _____

_____

3. _____

_____

4. _____

_____

5. _____

_____

_____ 1. _____

_____

2. _____

_____

3. _____

_____

4. _____

_____

5. _____

_____

16

PERSONAL OR CIVIC ACCOMPLISHMENTS

NAME _____   DATE _____

Your Title (if any), Organization, City, and State
_____ 1. _____
    Period in years
                          _____

                       2. _____

                          _____

                       3. _____

                          _____

_____ 1. _____

                          _____

                       2. _____

                          _____

                       3. _____

                          _____

_____ 1. _____

                          _____

                       2. _____

                          _____

                       3. _____

                          _____

CAREER GOALS

NAME _____   DATE _____

Goal	Immediate	In 5 years	In 10 years
Position			
Salary			
Perquisites			
Percent equity			
Scope of Authority			
Number of subordinates, direct			
Number of subordinates, indirect			
Independence			
Structured environment			
Work hours vs. private time			
Travel			
Percent time working with--People			
Data			
Things			
Security			
Challenge			
Professional recognition			
Civic recognition			
Personal recognition			

MARKETING TARGETS

NAME _____   DATE _____

   I. Industry _____
      Size of organization _____
      Type of organization _____
      Geographical area _____
      Position and responsibilities _____
      _____
      Personal preference _____
      Career preference _____

  II. Industry _____
      Size of organization _____
      Type of organization _____
      Geographical area _____
      Position and responsibilities _____
      _____
      Personal preference _____
      Career preference _____

 III. Industry _____
      Size of organization _____
      Type of organization _____
      Geographical area _____
      Position and responsibilities _____
      _____
      Personal preference _____
      Career preference _____

  IV. Industry _____
      Size of organization _____
      Type of organization _____
      Geographical area _____
      Position and responsibilities _____
      _____
      Personal preference _____
      Career preference _____

PERSONAL RESUME FORM

Photo

Name: _____

Address: _____
_____

Telephone: _____

Civil Status: _____
_____

Children: _____

Education: Graduate _____
_____
_____
_____

University _____
_____
_____
_____
_____

Continuing Education _____
_____
_____
_____
_____

Professional Highlights:
_____
_____
_____
_____
_____
_____
_____
_____
_____
_____
_____
_____
_____
_____

19

PERSONAL RESUME FORM

Professional History:

PERSONAL RESUME FORM

Professional History:

19

PERSONAL RESUME FORM

Professional Organizations: _____
_____
_____
_____
_____

Military Service: _____
_____
_____
_____

Special Items of Interest: _____
_____
_____
_____
_____
_____
_____
_____
_____
_____
_____
_____
_____
_____
_____
_____

References: _____
_____
_____
_____
_____

PERSONAL RESUME
March 1977

Photo

NAME: NAFF, William G.

ADDRESS: 1674 North Park Drive
                    Atlanta, Georgia 30341
TELEPHONE: (404) 936-7511

CIVIL STATUS: Born November 6, 1923, Decatur, Georgia; married.

CHILDREN: Two daughters, both graduates of the University of
                    Georgia.

EDUCATION: University—-Graduated in 1951 from the University of
                    Georgia, School of Commerce and Business Administration,
                    with a Bachelor of Science degree; majored in Accounting.

                    Continuing Education—-Have completed university courses in
                    Income Tax Procedure, Principles of Management, and Com-
                    puter Programming as well as other courses in computer
                    use, accounting, and speed reading.

PROFESSIONAL   As Treasurer or Controller of four companies ranging in
HIGHLIGHTS: size from $500,000 to over $40 million in annual sales,
                    implemented and designed systems for conversion of all ac-
                    counting functions to computer application including work
                    with minicomputers, service bureaus, large systems, and
                    conversion from one computer to another. Designed and
                    established an inventory control system at a franchise
                    operation which reduced inventory requirements by 35%
                    or $500,000. In cash control, set up and managed an
                    investment portfolio which increased after tax profits by
                    $25,000. Designed a credits control system for a grocery
                    distributor which reduced credits issued by $2,500 per
                    week. Cut delinquent account period by one-half for
                    installment sales at a multicemetery operation.

PROFESSIONAL HISTORY:
Chicken Quick Food Company, Inc., Atlanta, Georgia
1973-1977   After a 9-month break in statements, joined this $12-
                    million-gross-sales franchise food operation as Treasurer
                    and Controller. Brought all records up to date and com-
                    pleted annual audit and 10-K SEC filing in less than three
                    months working with predominantly new staff. Replaced
                    minicomputer with a service bureau including design of the
                    system for all accounting functions. Recognized need and
                    set up a formal Buyer's Guide showing inventory movement,
                    source, and delivery information. This allowed a 50%
                    reduction in purchasing and staff. Established a system
                    for control of accounts receivable which reduced bad debts
                    from $85,000 to $40,000 annually. Designed and wrote
                    accounting systems for franchisees.

Cooperative Grocers of North Georgia, Inc., Atlanta, Georgia

1972–1973   As Controller of this $43 million cooperative food distributor, put accounts payable and general ledger on computer. Implemented rigid inventory control system which reduced inventory losses by $30,000 the first year and reduced inventory level by $1/4 million. This also improved accuracy of inventory records allowing gradual reduction in physical inventory count period from monthly to semiannually. Became Controller and set up complete accounting systems for three new subsidiary acquisitions in advertising, radio broadcasting, and maintenance.

Zigler Foods Company, Inc., Tallahassee, Florida

1971   As Treasurer and Controller of this wholesale grocery company, converted over 150 computer programs from an IBM 360 to a Burroughs B–2500 system in less than four weeks. Set up a retail accounting system for company stores and revamped the billing, inventory control, and purchase order systems. After establishing a computer accounting system, contracted with a local television station to process its daily program analysis producing additional revenue of $18,000 per year with no increase in costs.

Mark Memorial Services, Inc., Atlanta, Georgia

1956–1968   Treasurer and Controller of this $500,000 cemetery company with operations in five Southeastern cities. Set up and operated accounting system for both the home office and all local offices. Personally wrote 80% of the programs to computerize accounts. Set up installment sales accounting procedures including an automatic delinquent notice system which reduced average delinquent time by one-half from 20 to 10 days.

Civil Service, Atlanta and College Park, Georgia

1949–1956   Served as Accountant, City Clerk, and Treasurer for the Atlanta Board of Health and the City of College Park, Georgia.

MILITARY
SERVICE: Served in the U.S. Navy from 1940 to 1946; honorably discharged with the rank of Yeoman 1st Class.

OTHER: Was a founder and first treasurer of the accounting fraternity at the University of Georgia.

REFERENCES: Mr. K. R. Greenfield, Manager, Atlanta Data Center, Compushare, Inc., Atlanta, Georgia, (404) 938–6811.

     Mr. Michael Strong, Vice-President, Southern National Bank of Atlanta, Atlanta, Georgia, (404) 577–3681.

     Mr. Earle Barker, CPA, Howard, Barker and McDowell, Atlanta, Georgia, (404) 233–5967.

PERSONAL RESUME
February 1977

| | | Photo |

NAME: MARQUE, Ronald J.
(Pronounced "Mark")

ADDRESS: Apartment 4, Terrace Court
Chicago, Illinois 47092

TELEPHONE: (312) 221-9130

CIVIL STATUS: Born May 30, 1950, Pottstown, Pennsylvania; U.S. citizen;
married.

LANGUAGES: Both English and French spoken, read, and written
fluently.

EDUCATION: Graduated from the University of Illinois in 1976 with a
Master of Business Administration degree in Finance and
Econometrics. In addition to normal business courses,
studied business applications of statistics including
queuing theory, Markov chains, and variance and regression
analysis. Studied econometric modeling, investment
analysis, and corporate finance and planning.

Received a Bachelor of Arts degree in Political Science
with a minor in Economics also from the University of
Illinois in 1972.

Continuing Education: Completed the American Institute of
Real Estate Appraisers initial course on real estate appraising.

PROFESSIONAL   For a $500 million mortgage company, instituted and compu-
HIGHLIGHTS: terized regression analysis for loan closings and interest
rate movements with 88% accuracy in gross amounts and 100%
accuracy in predicting trends. As head of the marketing
department, produced $600,000 of profit in mortgage sales
while the money market fluctuated through two complete
reversals. Made discount decisions in conjunction with
the president that resulted in an increase in production
of 100.9%. Analyzed and originated the sale of mortgage-
backed securities, producing profits of up to $57,000 per
security. Reorganized the marketing department, resulting
in an 18% decrease in total expense and 80% decrease in
overtime.

PROFESSIONAL HISTORY:

Ingel Mortgage Company, Inc., Chicago, Illinois

1974-1976
As head of the marketing department, sold a two-year inventory of $1.5 million of mortgages with poor payment histories. Sold over $1 million of Florida condominiums in the recession year of 1975 with a $27,000 profit. Re-negotiated a $1 million commitment which was in jeopardy. Analyzed and corrected a mortgage portfolio of an acquired subsidiary to meet GNMA requirements. Set up computer control of GNMA tandem commitments for $86 million of mortgages. Analyzed and underwrote all conventional loans from ten company branches.

1973-1974
As collection department head, decreased delinquency under 4% for the first time in three years. Reorganized work-load of seven staff members for optimum effectiveness. Reorganized delinquent files and created computer print-out cards for improved accuracy and quick retrieval.

American Financial Services, Grove Heights, Illinois

1972-1973
As customer service representative for this small loan service company, was able to collect over $2,000 of ac-counts which had been written off as bad debts. Had best delinquency ratio on consumer accounts and under 1% on dealer accounts. Responsible for analyzing and closing both second mortgage and personal secured loans.

Barbara Corporation, Pottstown, Pennsylvania

Summers:

1968-1971
As a machinist in the largest plant of this industrial manufacturer, ran eight different metal-working and milling machines on a universal-joint production line. Worked seven days a week through each summer to earn 65% of college expenses.

PROFESSIONAL
ORGANIZATIONS: Association of MBA Executives

REFERENCES:
Ms. Connie H. Thomason, Vice-President, Ingel Mortgage Company, Chicago, Illinois, (312) 251-2447.

Mr. Ralph G. Brown, Manager, CIT Financial Services, Grove Heights, Illinois, (312) 823-3100.

Mr. Michael Padalarno, Vice-President, Ingel Mortgage Company, Chicago, Illinois, (312) 251-2447.

PERSONAL RESUME
April 1977

Photo

NAME: SHOOKLER, Lewis B.

ADDRESS: 365 Poinsettia Drive
                Wilmington, Delaware 19804

TELEPHONE: (302) 879-6685

CIVIL STATUS: Born September 10, 1934, Chicago, Illinois; married.

CHILDREN: Five daughters, ranging in age from 6 to 19.

PROFESSIONAL   As sales representative or assistant manager for four con-
HIGHLIGHTS: sumer product companies ranging in size from $14 million
                to $150 million in annual sales, had nine consecutive
                years of sales increases. Won three individual sales
                awards. Worked closely with outside consulting firm on
                improved reporting system and developed new merchandising
                programs which resulted in doubling department exposure in
                major accounts. Successfully opened 71 accounts for a new
                product line in less than two years. Took over a terri-
                tory and increased sales 48% in the first five months
                while adding 37 new accounts. Screened and then field-
                trained 12 salesmen for the Middle Atlantic region with
                resultant increase in sales of over 25%.

PROFESSIONAL HISTORY:
Woman's World, Inc., New York, New York
1975-1977   As territory salesman for Delaware, Maryland, and Southern
                New Jersey with this national apparel company, sold
                merchandise to 168 medium to better specialty shops and
                department stores including 90 of the 97 key accounts in
                cities of 5,000 population and above. Increased territory
                sales 10% for fiscal 1976, against a 3% company increase.
                Reestablished line into major position at the first and
                third largest department store chains in the area and in-
                creased volume 32% in second largest chain.

Balanchine, Inc., Wilmington, Delaware
1974-1975   As assistant store manager in the second largest branch of
                this major Delaware department store chain, supervised 108
                salespeople and service clerks. Personally handled all
                customer complaints. Suggested and implemented relocation
                of sportswear and cosmetic departments, contributing to
                the growth of this store from fifth to second largest in
                the chain. Took personal supervision of intimate apparel
                department, resulting in its becoming largest in sales
                compared with 21 other stores.

Poyner, Gross, Inc., Wilmington, Delaware
1973-1974   As president and minority stockholder of this new commer-
              cial and residential decoration service company, was
              responsible for initial organization and for establishing
              bank credit lines. Personally generated $65,000 sales
              volume in first four months. Recruited and trained four
              office and sales employees.

Elen Shoreman, Inc., New York, New York
1970-1973   In three Middle Atlantic states as salesman for complete
              intimate and career apparel lines, increased annual sales
              from $236,000 to $425,000 in two years. Saw potential new
              market and opened 11 military exchanges for the foundation
              line. Worked with cross-selling of mixed product lines
              and introduced a completely new line for the firm.

Rothman's, Inc., Division of ITC, Inc., New York
1958-1970   Increased sales from $286,000 to $636,000 in an already
              developed market when territory salesman in Delaware and
              Southern New Jersey. Led the Middle Atlantic region in
              sales two of the three years it led the nation for the
              company. Also handled sales interviews and screening for
              all applicants in Trenton and Wilmington.

EDUCATION: Attended Joliet College, Joliet, Ohio, 1954-1956, with
              continuing education in Psychology and Commercial Law at
              night. Completed the Xerox Corporation Sales Training
              Course.

MILITARY   Served nine years in the Illinois and Delaware Air Na-
SERVICE: tional Guard, including one year active duty. Honorably
              discharged with rank of Staff Sergeant.

REFERENCES: Mr. John Barton, Executive Vice-President, Rothman's,
              Inc., New York, New York, (212) 782-1444.

              Ms. Bernice Strutz, Merchandise Manager, Lower's Depart-
              ment Store, Wilmington, Delaware, (302) 263-0344.

              Mr. Milton Blatt, V/P National Sales Manager, Elen Shore-
              man, Inc., New York, New York, (212) 867-9700.

PERSONAL RESUME
April 1977

NAME: HARLEN, Carter M.   Photo

ADDRESS: 3230 West Valley Drive
                    New Orleans, Louisiana 70132
TELEPHONE: (504) 977-8815, home;
                    (504) 964-2340, office

CIVIL STATUS: Born March 15, 1933, New Orleans, Louisiana; U.S. citizen;
                    married.

CHILDREN: One son, 20; one daughter, 13.

EDUCATION: Graduated in 1962 from Anderson College, Anderson,
                    Michigan, with a Bachelor of Science degree. Major
                    subjects included Social Studies and Education; minors
                    were in English and Psychology.

GRADUATE
SCHOOL: Anderson School of Theology, Anderson, Michigan, 1963.

CONTINUING   University of Notre Dame, South Bend, Indiana, summer
EDUCATION: 1967; completed course in Public Relations and Administra-
                    tion for Colleges and Universities.

                    Robert Sharpe Institute, Memphis, Tennessee, 1967 and 1968;
                    completed Estate Planning and College Development courses.

PROFESSIONAL   Established the development department for a Midwestern
HIGHLIGHTS: liberal arts college and served as its development and
                    alumni officer. Raised over $1 million in deferred gifts
                    for endowment and organized special campaigns to build a
                    new administrative building costing $3.5 million. Served
                    as executive director for a permanent, fund-raising orga-
                    nization of 13 Midwestern graduate seminaries. Increased
                    member schools from 7 to 13 and set up a corporate fund
                    campaign that increased gifts from business by 95%.
                    Served as pastor of a community church and vice-chairman
                    for research and development of a state board of church
                    extensions. Served as president of a real estate develop-
                    ment corporation.

PROFESSIONAL   Fund Raising
EXPERIENCE: As development and alumni director at Anderson College,
                    Anderson, Michigan, reorganized entire department and
                    instituted business procedures for all functions.
                    Established gift records and prospect files and increased
                    regular contributions over three times. Planned,
                    contracted, and raised funds for a $3.5 million building.
                    Assisted with estate planning as a major fund-raising
                    technique with potential bequests exceeding $4 million.

As executive director of the Accredited Theological
Schools of Michigan and Indiana, planned, organized, and
implemented multi—seminary fund—raising activities that
increased the number of contributors by 65%. Increased
school membership and total contributed dollars and obtained largest single gift in the organization's history.

Was planning and development consultant for Sanford Southern College, Lake City, Florida, and for an international
church radio and television commission. Established a
five—year, long—range plan for the college including fund-
raising and deferred—giving programs that increased gift
income 40%.

Ministry
Pastored a community church, increasing its regular atten-
dance by 267%, its annual regular income by 375%, and its
net assets by 350%.

As vice—chairman of a state board of church extensions,
was responsible for research and development. Made
logistical studies for six areas and provided consultant
services to churches for design, construction, financing,
and fund raising.

Business
As owner/president of a land development company in
Central Florida, purchased and sold 497 building lots;
purchased, developed, and sold a seven—unit shopping
plaza.

PROFESSIONAL   American College Public Relations Association
ORGANIZATIONS: American Alumni Council
                    New Orleans Board of Realtors
                    Church of God, Anderson, Michigan, Ordained Minister.

REFERENCES: Dr. John Dickhaught, President
                    Methodist Theological School of Michigan
                    Columbus, Michigan 49605
                    Telephone (313) 363—1247

                    Dr. Hilda Rich, Director
                    Motivation Center, Inc.
                    New Orleans, Louisiana 70717
                    Telephone (504) 933—2416

                    Dr. John Knight, President
                    United Theological Seminary
                    Dayton, Michigan 48327
                    Telephone (313) 279—5717

PERSONAL RESUME
January 1977

Photo

NAME: BROOKS, Jerrold A.

ADDRESS: 1216 Thornhill Drive
                   Dallas, Texas 75221
TELEPHONE: (214) 871-1496

CIVIL STATUS: Born April 12, 1929, Columbus, Ohio; married.

CHILDREN: One daughter, age 13; three sons, ages 4, 11, and 15.

EDUCATION: University--Graduated from the University of Ohio in 1951
                   with a Bachelor of Science degree in Business Administra-
                   tion; majored in Production Management. Minor subjects
                   included Engineering, Accounting, and Statistics.
                   Continuing Education--Mechanical Engineering, University
                   of Texas, 1955-1959; have also completed courses and
                   seminars in Quality Control, Packaging, Textiles,
                   Purchasing, Time and Motion Study, Accounting,
                   Investments, Real Estate, and Public Speaking.

PROFESSIONAL   In 23 years with Howard & Sharpe, a $25-million, five-
HIGHLIGHTS: plant manufacturer of children's through juniors' sports
                   and outerwear, served variously as vice-president or
                   manager over Marketing, Merchandising, Packaging,
                   Manufacturing, Engineering, Quality Control, and Purchas-
                   ing. Significant accomplishments included performing most
                   new product and trend research while serving on a four-man
                   merchandising committee for 15 years; determined each
                   style that was adopted for a given line. Sales increased
                   from $3.5 million to $25 million and profits from $300,000
                   to $1,800,000. Set up and managed first Southern plant.
                   Designed, built, and managed a 200-man packaging depart-
                   ment; developed packaging design and procedures for the
                   entire diversified product line. Developed work-flow sys-
                   tems in outerwear plant, producing savings of $50,000 per
                   year. Originated quality control program for the entire
                   company, reducing losses and returns by $200,000 per year.
                   Developed company reorganization and cost reduction
                   program in 1974 that saved over $500,000 in two years.

PROFESSIONAL   Merchandising and Marketing: From selling on the road to
EXPERIENCE: recruiting and managing the entire sales force, have par-
                   ticipated in all areas of sales, advertising, garment
                   design, and merchandising. Put company into jacket and
                   carcoat field, increasing outerwear sales 300%. Developed
                   entry into perma-press field with resultant 70% increase
                   in sportswear sales over two years. Pursued and nego-
                   tiated highly profitable Army contracts during Viet Nam
                   period. Handled customer service with large discount
                   chains, increasing sales 20%. Was responsible for sales
                   projections and costing for a complete, diversified line.

Packaging: Originated, developed, and directed a "total" finishing and packaging program for the entire family from 1962-1974. Designed every package in the diversified line in coordination with the marketing/merchandising plans. Responsible for all labeling, tagging, logo design, brand coordination, advertising gimmicks, and promotional programs. Developed color hanger concept for selection of coordinated sets at retail level.

Production and Engineering: Developed and set up a complete perma-press line, including all material handling. Supervised design and construction for four major plant expansions, including layout of all production machinery. Improved methods of pattern making, fit control, spreading, and cutting, which saved $100,000 in three years. Started up and managed two new plant facilities. Originated, designed, and set up quality control laboratory. Have worked with time studies, production costs and rates, cost formulas, production control, and planning. Have operated all machines and entire production facilities personally.

Purchasing: Managed purchasing effort over a five-year period with peak annual level of $6 million. Negotiated contracts with major textile suppliers, saving $50,000 in one year measured against going market prices and purchases of similar goods and quantities in previous year. Organized complete quality "spec" system used in large contracts, backed up by fabric inspection system at plants and lab. This improved quality of fabrics and garments and saved $40,000 in fabrics, $10,000 in trim, and up to $50,000 per year on customer returns. Familiar with textile market trends, price movements in greige goods, blends, cottons, and other fibers, as well as dyeing, printing, and finishing markets.

Administration: Managed building construction and real estate; headed budget committee and cost accounting departments. Did research in cost control and overhead reduction, resulting in increased profits of 3% to 4% in one year due only to savings produced. Set up traffic department with freight scheduling and cost control, saving in excess of $50,000 per year. Participated in or managed all administrative functions of the company.

REFERENCES: Mr. Samuel Bayer, President, Warner Thread Company, New York, New York, (212) 938-0424.

Mr. Sam Norwood, Vice-President, Howard & Sharpe, Dallas, Texas, Office (214) 925-3771; Home (214) 870-2142.

Mr. Alan Sherman, President, Sherman Plastics Company, New York, New York, (212) 760-8870.

PERSONAL RESUME
May 1977

NAME: PARSONS, Janet C.

ADDRESS: 2701 Flagstone Road
                    Kansas City, Missouri 64112
TELEPHONE: (816) 533-2069

CIVIL STATUS: Born September 30, 1936, in Valley View, Kansas; married.

CHILDREN: One son, age 11; twin daughters, age 13.

EDUCATION: Graduate--Received law degree, L.L.B., from the Univer-
                    sity of Missouri in 1963; admitted to the Missouri Bar
                    that same year.

                    University--Graduated from Cornell University in 1958 with
                    a Bachelor of Arts degree in Political Science.

                    Continuing Education--Have taken over 20 University- and
                    Bar-sponsored courses and seminars in various aspects of
                    continuing legal education but predominantly related to
                    real estate. Completed real estate brokers test require-
                    ments and am licensed as a Missouri real estate broker.

PROFESSIONAL   Nine years of general law practice as a sole practitioner
HIGHLIGHTS: and managing partner in Salina, Missouri, followed by five
                    years of corporate experience predominantly related to
                    real estate matters as senior title attorney with Associ-
                    ates Title Insurance Company in Kansas City, Missouri.

                    In general practice, formed over a dozen corporations;
                    handled 15 real estate litigation cases; negotiated set-
                    tlements and tried various tort claims; acted as a trustee
                    in bankruptcy and served as general guardian and general
                    administrator of Columbia County, Missouri. In corporate
                    experience, am usually assigned the more difficult real
                    estate title cases and examinations. As only lawyor in
                    office with trial experience, have handled or been con-
                    sulted on all cases involving claims in Missouri. Prepare
                    and administer escrow contracts, solicit new business, and
                    disburse construction funds.

PROFESSIONAL HISTORY:
1972-Present   Associates Title Insurance Company, Kansas City, Mis-
                    souri--As senior title attorney in this 40-person office
                    with five lawyers, have examined over 4,000 real estate
                    titles of up to $20 million value. Make decisions con-
                    cerning insurability and underwriting and draft insurance

contracts and binders. Have handled claims concerning a wide variety of real-estate-related disputes resulting in both negotiated settlements and court trials. Work daily with between three to eight private and outside corporate attorneys on real estate and real-estate-related matters. Evaluate hazards, set limits, draft and administer escrow accounts. Responsible for disbursement of multimillion-dollar construction funds; have settled disputes over and established safeguards against mechanics' and materialmen's liens; meet regularly with real estate agents, bank and lending institutions' loan officials, developers, and other lawyers to discuss real estate projects and to solicit business. Have worked with property sales, transfers, trades, leases, development, zoning, uses, condemnations, and mineral rights.

1963–1972   General Law Practice, Salina, Missouri
General practice in this small city serving a population of 60,000 with 30 to 40 lawyers. Was general guardian and general administrator for the county from 1963 to 1971. Handled over 30 estates in this capacity including both sale and purchase of real estate for wards. In corporate work, formed, amended, merged, and dissolved over a dozen corporate charters. Handled over 15 cases of real estate litigation including judicial sales, bankruptcy, bills to quiet title, condemnation for both state and defendants, boundary disputes, foreclosures, and liens. Drafted and negotiated wide variety of contracts including labor union contracts. Tried and won a trademark infringement and unfair business practices suit. Have negotiated, tried, and won a number of tort cases.

PROFESSIONAL   President of the Columbia County Bar Association in 1968–
ORGANIZATIONS: 1969. Currently a member of the American, Missouri, and
                Kansas City Bar Associations and the Sigma Delta Kappa
                legal fraternity.

SPECIAL ITEM   Conducted Real Estate Seminar for the University of
OF INTEREST: Missouri Continuing Legal Education Program.

REFERENCES: Mr. James M. Spence, Jr.; Pelham, McDaniel and Jones,
                Kansas City, Missouri, (816) 824-9523.

                Mr. Elton G. Brown, III; Circuit Judge, Maclenny,
                Missouri, (314) 752-7389.

                Mr. Thomas O. Paulson; Hughes, Coretti, Forrester, Rudd
                and Hensley, Kansas City, Missouri, (816) 251-5050.

26

REFERENCE CHECK QUESTIONNAIRE

Reference's name _____   Date _____
Title _____
Company _____   City _____
Telephone number _____   State _____

1. How long have you known him? _____
2. In what capacity have you known him? _____
3. How did he perform in his job? _____
   _____
4. Is he a hard worker? _____
5. How intelligent is he? _____
6. How original or imaginative? _____
7. How aggressive? _____
8. How egotistical? _____
9. How versatile? _____
10. How much potential does he have? _____
    _____
11. How does he get along with superiors and subordinates? _____
    _____
12. Does he take criticism well? _____
    _____
13. Can he be demanding of his subordinates? _____
    _____
14. Does he have a sense of humor? _____
15. Does he tolerate frustration well? _____
16. Is he honest? _____
17. _____
    _____
18. _____
    _____
19. What are his weaknesses or negative points? _____
    _____
20. Would you consider hiring him yourself? _____

General comments concerning this call and the reference _____
_____
_____
_____
_____

27

William G. Naff
1674 North Park Drive
Atlanta, Georgia 30341
Telephone (404) 936-7511

March 15, 1977

Mr. K. R. Greenfield
Manager
Compushare, Inc.
2117 First Avenue, North
Atlanta, Georgia 30308

Dear Kirk:

I enjoyed seeing you again after so many months and particularly
appreciate your willingness to be a reference in my current job campaign.
As promised, I enclose a copy of my resume.

My objective is to find a position as treasurer or vice-president of
finance with a medium-size to large manufacturing company. I feel my
experience with distributors is readily transferable to other companies
which have large inventory and data processing operations.

I will keep you informed of my progress. If convenient, you might call to
advise me of any companies that contact you. This will help me plan my
strategy.

My best regards to Nancy and the children.

Yours truly,

William G. Naff

Enclosure

PERSONAL CONTACTS LIST

NAME _____   DATE _____

_____   Name _____   Date Contacted _____ by letter,
                                               phone, meeting _____
            Title _____   Follow-up _____
            Company _____   _____
            Address _____   _____
            City and state _____   _____
            Telephone _____   _____

Lewis B. Shookler
365 Poinsettia Drive
Wilmington, Delaware 19804
Telephone (302) 879-6685

April 15, 1977

Mr. William M. Morris
Head Buyer
Waldon Department Stores, Inc.
1345 5th Avenue, North
Wilmington, Delaware 19899

Dear Bill:

    Thank you for your time last Wednesday and your kind offer of
assistance in my search for a new job.

    As we discussed, I am now ready to move out of territory work into
sales management. With my depth of experience in the apparel field, I
can make a contribution to any clothing or related manufacturer interested in increasing sales in the Delaware, Maryland, and New Jersey area.

    In particular, my knowledge of the 97 key accounts in this area and
my sales training experience should be of interest. The enclosed copy of
my resume includes some of my other sales accomplishments.

    Following your suggestion, I plan to contact Roger Harris of Simon
and Harris next week. I would appreciate your passing my resume on to
other potentially interested companies or advising me of contacts I might
make. I will let you know what Mr. Harris says and will keep you advised
of my progress.

Cordially,

Lewis B. Shookler

LBS/js
Enclosure

Lewis B. Shookler
365 Poinsettia Drive
Wilmington, Delaware 19804
Telephone (302) 879-6685

April 15, 1977

Mr. Glen S. Brunstein, President
Made-to-Form, Incorporated
1400 Madison Avenue
New York, New York 10010

Dear Glen:

Confirming our telephone conversation yesterday, I enclose my
resume. Your assistance in my job search should be of great help.

I am now interested in moving out of direct sales into a position as
regional sales manager for an apparel firm. My preference is to stay in
the Wilmington area where I can make maximum use of my contacts with over
160 retail outlet buyers.

Although you had no immediate suggestions, please look over my
resume and keep my availability in mind. I will plan to call you again
in about two weeks to advise you of my progress and check on any ideas
you may have.

Yours truly,

Lewis B. Shookler

LBS/js
Enclosure

Lewis B. Shookler
365 Poinsettia Drive
Wilmington, Delaware 19804
Telephone (302) 879-6685

April 20, 1977

Mr. Benjamin R. Erdman
Senior Vice-President
Lovejoy Clothes, Inc.
1791 Peachtree Street
Richmond, Virginia 23224

Dear Mr. Erdman:

Confirming our telephone conversation yesterday, I enclose a copy of my resume.

As Mr. Roger Harris explained to you, I am looking for a regional sales manager's position with an apparel company. Your firm may be in a position to use a man with my background and experience.

As you will see in my resume, I have a history of increasing territory sales in both difficult and well-established markets. During 1976 I led company sales for Woman's World with a 10% increase versus a 3% increase nationwide. I also trained Middle-Atlantic-region salesmen for Rothman's and increased territory volume over 25%.

I will call you late next week to schedule a personal interview. I am in Richmond frequently and could meet with you at your convenience.

Yours truly,

Lewis B. Shookler

REGIONAL SALES MANAGER

We are looking for a person with strong sales background in the apparel field to head up one of our major regions. Supervisory and sales training experience are required. Reply with your resume and salary history to Box 147. Our employees know of this search. We are an equal opportunity employer.

Lewis B. Shookler
365 Poinsettia Drive
Wilmington, Delaware 19804
Telephone (302) 879-6685

April 28, 1977

Box 147
c/o Woman's Wear Journal
964 Avenue of the Americas
New York, New York 10010

Dear Sirs:

As sales representative or assistant manager for four national
apparel and department store companies, I have 17 years of experience
including a continuous record of year-to-year volume increases and a 93%
penetration of total key accounts in my territory.

Because you advertised for a regional sales manager with a strong
background in the apparel field, you might be interested in some of my
other accomplishments.

--As a territory salesman for Woman's World, Inc., I successfully
   opened 71 accounts for a new leisure-wear line in less than two
   years.
--I took over another territory and increased sales 48% in the first
   five months while adding 37 new outlets.
--For the Middle Atlantic region, I screened and then field-trained 12
   new salesmen with a resultant increase in sales of over 25% for
   intimate apparel.
--I suggested and implemented relocation of sportswear, lingerie, and
   cosmetics departments in a department store branch of Balanchine,
   Inc., moving this outlet from fifth to second largest in the chain.
--During this period, I supervised 108 department store salespeople.
--I saw a potential new market and opened 11 military exchanges for a
   foundation line for Elen Shoreman, Inc.

I am 43 years old, married, with five daughters, ages 6 to 19.
Though I have a slight preference for the Middle Atlantic region or the
Northeast, I am more attracted by professional challenge.

I would like to discuss further details of my experience with you in
a personal interview and can be reached at the above number.

Yours truly,

Lewis B. Shookler

FINANCIAL ANALYST
Requirements include advanced mathematics, familiarity with computer techniques, 2 to 5 years experience in corporate financial analysis, and a college degree, MBA preferred. Salary to $20,000, potential for advancement, and excellent benefits. Send your resume in confidence to:

Northwest Instruments Company
P.O. Box 2515
Portland, Oregon 97201

We Are an Equal
Opportunity Employer

Note:

The respondent to this ad—Ronald J. Marque—had little experience in his target field. He therefore emphasized his education in the first paragraph of his letter and wrote his accomplishments in mortgage sales to relate to financial analysis. Refer to his resume (#21).

Ronald J. Marque
Apartment 4, Terrace Court
Chicago, Illinois 47092
Telephone (312) 221-9130

February 11, 1977

Mr. Brian M. Cooper
Vice-President, Finance
Northwest Instruments Company
P.O. Box 2515
Portland, Oregon 97201

Dear. Mr. Cooper:

For a $500-million mortgage company, I instituted and computerized a regression analysis for loan closings and interest rate movements with 88% accuracy in gross amount and 100% accuracy in predicting trends. I am a 26-year-old MBA graduate in Finance and Econometrics. In addition to usual business courses, I studied business application of statistics including queuing theory, Markov chains, variance and regression analysis, as well as modeling, investment analysis, and corporate planning.

Because you advertised for a financial analyst with this type of experience and training, I thought you would be interested in some of my other accomplishments.

--For the management of the Ingel Mortgage Company, I analyzed and wrote reports on a system to predict sales volume for cash management, a history and evaluation of unsold mortgage loans, and an audit report on the portfolio of an acquired subsidiary.

--Using internal rate of return, discounted cash flow, payback period, and lease vs. buy, I performed a number of capital investment case studies ranging in size from $10,000 to $600,000.

--I performed special analytical studies and financial modeling for various company functions as well as ascertaining federal mortgage auction results using computer techniques.

--I analyzed and originated the sale of mortgage-backed securities, producing profits of up to $57,000 per security.

--As a department head, I reorganized the mortgage marketing function, resulting in an 18% decrease in total expense and an 80% decrease in overtime with no loss of efficiency.

I am married with no children and have worked for two mortgage and finance companies. My objective is to find a position outside the mortgage field where I can make better application of my training and recent business experience.

I would like to discuss further details of my background and accomplishments with you in a personal interview. After 5:00 P.M. I can be reached at the above number, or at (312) 967-4960 during working hours.

Yours truly,

Ronald J. Marque

VICE PRESIDENT AND
GENERAL MANAGER

The largest women's tailored-suit and dress manufacturer in the United States needs a "hands on" executive to take full profit-and-loss responsibility over its Columbus, South Carolina, division. Minimum 10 years apparel experience including both marketing and production. Salary commensurate with experience.

You must submit your complete resume and salary requirements in order to be considered.

Reply to: P.O. Box 19711
New York, N.Y. 10022
We Are an Equal Opportunity
Employer

Note:

The respondent to this ad — Jerrold A. Brooks — found the company's name by calling several friends to inquire about the identity of the largest tailored-suit manufacturer in the United States.

Jerrold A. Brooks
1216 Thornhill Drive
Dallas, Texas 75221
Telephone (214) 871-1496

February 6, 1977

Mr. Richard A. Graffner, Jr.
President
Liberty Tailored Wear, Inc.
P.O. Box 19711
New York, New York 10022

Dear Mr. Graffner:

As a vice-president of Howard & Sharpe, a children's and infants' apparel company, I performed new product and trend R&D while serving on a four-man merchandising committee for 15 years. Sales went from $3.5 million to $25 million and profits from $300,000 to $1.8 million.

Because you advertised for a vice-president and general manager over your Columbus, South Carolina, division, you may be interested in the scope of my experience and accomplishments.

--I started up and managed two new plant facilities and improved methods of pattern making, fit control, spreading, and cutting. This saved $100,000 in three years.
--I organized and implemented a complete quality "spec" system including fabric inspection and labs. This improved quality of fabrics and garments, saving $40,000 in fabrics, $10,000 in trim, and up to $50,000 per year in customer returns.
--With total responsibility over the marketing function, I changed to a more diversified and hi-styled line in sportswear in order to compete with cheap imports. Sales rose 40% in two years.
--Pioneering the color-hanger concept for selection of coordinated sets at retail, I also developed a packaging program including design of every package in the line.
--I have worked with time studies, production costs and rates, cost estimating formulas, production control, and production planning.

In am 47 years old and have a Business Administration degree with continuing education in Mechanical Engineering, Packaging, Textiles, Quality Control, and Accounting.

Although I do not have a current resume, I will be glad to prepare one to give you at an interview. I would like to meet with you to discuss my background in detail and will plan to call you late next week to see if a convenient time can be arranged.

Yours truly,

Jerrold A. Brooks

CORPORATE TREASURER

ICC has a key management opportunity for an individual with broad financial experience and specific expertise in treasury functions.

You will direct worldwide treasury activities. Primary responsibilities will be cash forecasting and managing bank relations, foreign currency exposure management, development of corporate financing strategies, and management of nonbenefit insurance programs.

This position requires a BS degree (MBA preferred) and 7 years experience in both controllership and treasury roles. Multinational responsibility is a prerequisite. The ideal candidate is currently earning 28 to 40K annually. This individual may be chief financial officer of a $20-million to $100-million company or treasurer or assistant treasurer of a $100-million-plus organization.

ICC is a multidivision, international electronics manufacturer headquartered in Los Angeles, CA. We reported record sales of $400 million, up 20% over last year.

For immediate and confidential consideration, please send your resume including salary history to: Doug Hooper, Director of Corporate Staffing, 464 West Street, Los Angeles, CA 94142. We are an equal opportunity employer m/f.

ICC CORPORATION

Note:

The respondent to this ad—Robert V. Blair—did not have the multinational experience that is a requirement in the advertisement. He simply did not mention it in his reply but referred directly to all other requirements. He added a paragraph that emphasized his qualifications in the areas requested and listed additional experience that should be of interest to the company.

ROBERT V. BLAIR
4177 Kennis Drive
Syracuse, New York 13209
Telephone (315) 881-0884

February 12, 1977

Mr. Doug Hooper
Director of Corporate Staffing
ICC Corporation
464 West Street
Los Angeles, California 94142

Dear Mr. Hooper:

I have been vice-president-finance of a $25-million company and assistant treasurer of a $400-million multidivision company. Because you advertised for a corporate treasurer with this type of background, you might be interested in some of my other accomplishments.

Cash Forecasting and Management. For Delta Materials Company, I developed and implemented major changes in a cash management system which produced a permanent reduction of "required cash balances" amounting to well over $1 million.

Bank Relations. I built and maintained rapport with bank contacts nationwide, which, at a critical time, allowed the doubling of credit lines in just three days, from $28 million to $57 million.

Corporate Financing. For Transport Systems, Inc., I negotiated private debt placements which increased long-term financing from $15 million to $38 million. I took part in the company's first public debt offering of $60 million and am also experienced in most other forms of financing.

Management of Insurance Programs. I held general corporate responsibility for these programs and was president of a subsidiary company which included a casualty insurance agency.

In addition to the above areas specifically mentioned in your advertisement, I have 13 years of experience in data processing, sales, and sales management with IBM Corporation. As Buffalo branch manager, I exceeded revenue and earnings objectives by 20%.

I am a Certified Public Accountant and holder of the Certificate in Management Accounting. I graduated from the University of Wisconsin in 1951 with a degree in Economics and Business with an Accounting major. I am 47 years old, married, and have two sons and two daughters, ages 8 to 20.

I would like to meet with you to discuss further details of my career and can be reached at the above number.

Sincerely,

Robert V. Blair

VP — INTERNATIONAL
In return for an opportunity to DOUBLE OUR INTERNATIONAL BUSINESS within three to five years, the successful candidate for our position of V.P. — International will send us a resume describing:

- concrete accomplishments
- prior P&L responsibility
- solid familiarity from within the controls industry
- responsible line experience in two or more of:
   marketing
   manufacturing
   engineering
- finance experience (plus)
- international experience (a must)
- geographical limitations (if any)
- compensation history and requirements

This position reports to the president of a firm in a turnaround situation already on the upswing. This is not a job for someone who wants to preside gracefully over an already secure commercial empire, but for an executive whose history, not just his/her cover story, reveals a productive response to risk and challenge. You should currently earn between thirty and forty thousand dollars.

We are an equal opportunity employer.
Reply to Box H-72, The New York Times

Note:

The reply by R. Felix Thomason was slightly modified in that it responds to the listed requirements by repeating the entire list except for compensation history. The result for this JOBSEARCH client was an immediate request for an interview. Out of over 1,000 replies to this advertisement, our client learned that his letter was the only one that responded point by point to the qualifications requested.

R. Felix Thomason
1921 Forest Run Drive
Great Falls, Virginia 23322
Telephone (703) 775-6421

April 2, 1977

Box H-72
c/o The New York Times
Post Office Box 361400
New York, New York 10023

Gentlemen:

In response to your New York Times advertisement of March 20, 1977, for a vice-president-international, I think you will be interested in the following aspects of my career:

--Concrete accomplishments: After taking over as president I returned a brick manufacturing company to profitability in two years, starting from a $300,000 loss in 1974.
--Prior P&L responsibility: I have been president of two separate corporations grossing in excess of $5 million per year.
--Familiarity with controls industry: In both Europe and the United States, I purchased and installed industrial controls of all types in new plant and modernization projects.
--Responsible line experience in
Marketing. I set up, staffed, and managed a sales group in Europe for an engineering and construction company, including direct sales effort on my part, and produced $50 million in project sales in the second year.
Manufacturing. I was president of one capital-intensive and one labor-intensive company as well as construction superintendent and field engineer for chemical, paper, and light-industry plants.
Engineering. I am a graduate mechanical engineer and have served as both project manager and project engineer for industrial contracts.
--Finance experience: I set up both accounting and cost control systems, and negotiated commercial bank and SBA loans and open lines of credit.
--International experience: I've served four years in Europe with a European firm having minority American participation, doing both Eastern and Western European work; I read and speak French fluently. My wife is a French citizen.
--Geographical limitations: Although proximity to a large city is preferred, I have no limitations.

I am 38 years old, a graduate of Yale University, with four children, ages 4 to 16.

At your convenience, I am available for an interview.

Yours truly,

R. Felix Thomason

Jerrold A. Brooks
1216 Thornhill Drive
Dallas, Texas 75221
Telephone (214) 871-1496

February 16, 1977

Mr. Richard A. Graffner, Jr.
President
Liberty Tailored Wear, Inc.
Post Office Box 19711
New York, New York 10022

Dear Mr. Graffner:

Thank you for your telephone call and interest in my background and experience. As you requested, I enclose a copy of my resume.

My accomplishments during a 23-year history with Howard & Sharpe have prepared me to take on the general manager's position which we discussed. In particular, my quality control experience outlined under "Production and Engineering" will allow me to make an immediate contribution to the customer-return and customer-complaint problems you mentioned.

At Howard & Sharpe my current salary is $40,000 with an incentive bonus that was $5,000 last year. Although one of my reasons for considering a job change is a salary increase, an acceptable salary will depend more upon the challenge of the position and the future potential.

After you have had an opportunity to review the enclosed information, I would like to meet with you to discuss the position and the contribution I can make. I look forward to receiving your call after your trip to the West Coast next week.

Cordially,

Jerrold A. Brooks

38

The letter on the facing page was sent by a JOBSEARCH client to large, national companies taken from the Dun & Bradstreet directories. It was directed toward a vice-president-finance or treasurer's position. Note the letter from this same person directed toward a corporate treasurer's position in a smaller company (#39). Also note this man's advertisement response (#35).

ROBERT V. BLAIR
4177 Kennis Drive
Syracuse, New York 13209
Telephone (315) 881-0884

January 28, 1977

Name, Title
Company Name
Street Address
City, State, Zip Code

Dear Mr. ___:

As assistant treasurer of Delta Materials Company, I developed and implemented major changes in the cash management system which produced a permanent reduction of "required cash balances" amounting to over $1 million. Subsequently, I became vice-president-finance with Transport Systems, Inc., and applied the same techniques with similar results.

If you need a financial executive with this type of imagination, you may be interested in other highlights of my career:

--Realizing the need, I created an investment policy and used it to manage a short-term portfolio that reached a high of $45 million.
--I negotiated private debt placements which increased long-term financing by more than $20 million.
--After setting as an objective a 25% reduction in days of sales in receivables, I established a plan and coordinated efforts for the successful achievement of this goal.
--I organized and participated in preparations for a $60 million public debt offering which opened a new source of financing for the company.
--In 13 years of experience in data processing, sales, and sales management with IBM Corporation, I became Buffalo branch manager and exceeded revenue and earnings objectives by 20%.

I am 47 years old, married, and have two sons and two daughters, ages 8 to 20. I graduated from the University of Wisconsin in 1951 with a Bachelor of Arts degree in Economics and Business with an Accounting major. I am a Certified Public Accountant and, in addition, holder of the Certificate in Management Accounting.

I would like to meet with you to discuss further details of my career in relation to a possible contribution I would make to your firm. In a few days I will call you to arrange a convenient time to meet.

Sincerely,

Robert V. Blair

39

The letter on the facing page was sent to the owners and presidents of small to medium-size local companies taken from the chamber of commerce directory. In this letter the candidate defined the Certificate in Management Accounting because it would not be known to officials in small companies. Note the other letters from this same man (#35 and 38). Also, note the reference to the candidate's Buffalo trip.

ROBERT V. BLAIR
4177 Kennis Drive
Syracuse, New York 13209
Telephone (315) 881-0884

January 28, 1977

Name
Title
Company Name
Street Address
Buffalo, New York, Zip Code

Dear Mr. ___:

I have held sales and sales management positions with IBM Corporation,
including Buffalo branch manager with complete profit-and-loss
responsibility for a $5-million operation, which exceeded revenue and
earnings objectives by 20%.

If you need a general manager with this type of experience, you may be
interested in certain highlights of my career:

--As owner, I formed a new company including financing, supervision of
  construction, selection and hiring of personnel, advertising,
  marketing, and management. I brought sales to a $125,000 yearly
  level in four months.
--As assistant treasurer of Delta Materials, a large public company, I
  built and maintained rapport with bank contacts which allowed the
  doubling of credit lines in just three days.
--Serving as a vice-president for a $25-million company, I designed a
  materials control system for two divisions to eliminate stock
  outages and reduce investment in inventory by 30%.
--As president of a subsidiary company, I directed the change of
  truck-body production facilities to a production line concept,
  including review and approval of each phase. Production cost savings
  exceeded 10%.

I am 47 years old, married, and have two sons and two daughters, ages 8
to 20. I graduated from the University of Wisconsin in 1951 with a
Bachelor of Arts degree in Economics and Business. My major was in
Accounting with a minor in Industrial Management. I am a holder of the
Certificate in Management Accounting, a recognition of proficiency in
both management and financial skills

I plan to be in Buffalo during the week of March 1 and would like to meet
with you at that time to discuss further details of my career. If you
will call me at the above number, we can arrange a convenient time to
meet.

Sincerely,

Robert V. Blair

40

The letter on the facing page was sent to college and university presidents in the target area. Note the difference in wording and in the choice and order of the accomplishments in his letter directed toward charities (#41).

CARTER M. HARLEN
3230 West Valley Drive
New Orleans, Louisiana 70132
Telephone (504) 977-8815

April 8, 1977

Name
Title
University Name
Street Address
City, State, Zip Code

Dear ____:

As planning and development director at a 1,000-student liberal arts college, I analyzed the space needs, layout, and design for a new administration building and then raised $3.5 million to build it.

If you need this type of fund-raising talent, you might be interested in some of my other accomplishments:

> For Anderson College I established a college development department and raised over $1 million in deferred gifts.

> I reorganized the alumni department and increased regular contributions over three times.

> As a result of my efforts in planning, organizing, and implementing a multischool fund-raising activity, corporate contributions increased by 95% and total contributors by 65% for the accredited theological schools of Michigan and Indiana.

> I developed a long-range fund-raising plan for Sanford Southern College, increasing its gifts by 130% over a four-year period.

> After taking a series of courses in Estate Planning, I applied this expertise to establish various trusts and bequests for several charitable organizations.

I am 44 years old and have a Bachelor of Science degree in Social Studies and Education with postgraduate work in Public Relations, Administration, and College Development. I am interested in a planning and development position with an educational institution in the New Orleans area.

I would like to meet with you to discuss my qualifications and their application to your organization and can be reached at 964-2340, or after 5:00 P.M. at 977-8815.

Sincerely,

Carter M. Harlen

The next letter is similar to the preceding letter, but is directed toward charities.

CARTER M. HARLEN
3230 West Valley Drive
New Orleans, Louisiana 70132
Telehpone (504) 977-8815

April 8, 1977

Name
Title
Organization Name
Street Address
City, State, Zip Code

Dear ___:

At a nonprofit, charitable institution where I was development director,
I planned a capital donation program and raised $3.5 million to build a
new administration building.

Because you may need this type of fund-raising talent, you might be
interested in some of my other accomplishments:

> I planned, organized, and implemented a multi-institutional fund-
> raising activity and increased corporate contributions by 95% and
> total contributors by 65%.

> I set up a five-year, long-range fund-raising and deferred-giving
> plan that increased gift income by 40%.

> For a charitable institution, I established a development department
> and raised over $1 million in deferred gifts.

> As a consultant, I developed a long-range fund-raising plan for
> a Southern college, increasing its gifts by 130% over a four-year
> period.

> After taking a series of courses in Estate Planning, I applied this
> expertise to establish various trusts and bequests for several
> charitable organizations.

I am 44 years old and have a Bachelor of Science degree in Social Studies
and Education with postgraduate work in Public Relations Administration.
I am interested in a planning and development position with a charitable
or civic organization in the New Orleans area.

I would like to meet with you to discuss my qualifications and their
application to your organization and can be reached at 964-2340, or after
5:00 P.M. at 977-8815.

Sincerely,

Carter M. Harlen

The letter on the facing page was sent to local companies and to vice-presidents of sales or marketing in national companies with Columbus distributorships. Note that this candidate did not have a university degree but had attended college. His specific age, which was 54, is not mentioned. However, the ages of his children would indicate that it was between 45 and 50.

William M. Larson
2631 Mountain View Drive
Columbus, Ohio 43221
Telephone (614) 876-0548

March 25, 1977

Name
Title
Company
Street Address
City, State, Zip Code

Dear ___:

As general manager or sales manager for Philco distributors in seven locations, I was sent to problem areas. In each case, I increased both sales and profits, reorganized the salespersons and dealer groups, introduced training programs, and turned a smooth-running operation over to my successor.

If sales or distribution is a problem for your company, you should be interested in some of my specific accomplishments:

For a local appliance and electronics distributor, I organized a special products division, selected lines, established marketing plans, and created $1.4 million in sales at a 22.3% gross profit.

At Philco in Columbus, I reorganized bookkeeping, billing, warehousing, and inventory control and reduced operating expense by 5%. At the same time, I increased total sales volume while items representing $597,000 in previous annual sales were being removed from the lines offered.

I established strict criteria for dealer accounts in Little Rock, Arkansas, set up a sales training and evaluation program, increased volume from $665,000 to $2.8 million, and increased profit margin from 7% to 12% in three years.

I started my career in retail sales with Sears, Roebuck and Company, setting sales records in three different departments in four years.

I am married and have two daughters, 23 and 25. I studied Business Administration at Marshall University, with continuing education in both company- and university-sponsored sales management courses and seminars. I am interested in finding a sales management position in the Columbus area.

I would like to meet with you to discuss in more detail my background and the contribution that I might make to your company. Late next week I will plan to call you to see when a convenient time can be arranged.

Yours truly,

William M. Larson

Enclosures

43

William M. Larson
2631 Mountain View Drive
Columbus, Ohio 43221
Telephone (614) 876-0548

April 4, 1977

Mr. Martin W. Bircher
Vice-President of Personnel
Hitachi Television, Inc.
Post Office Box 1796
San Francisco, California 94371

Dear Mr. Bircher:

As requested in your letter of March 30, 1977, my completed
employment application is enclosed. In order to give you more
information about my past experience and accomplishments, I have also
attached a copy of my resume.

In particular, you might note the history of sales and profit
increases which I created for Philco during 23 years of steadily
increasing responsibilities.

After you have had an opportunity to review the enclosed
information, I would like to meet with you to discuss the contribution
that I can make to Hitachi. I look forward to hearing from you in the
next few weeks.

Yours truly,

William M. Larson

Enclosures

44

William G. Naff
1674 North Park Drive
Atlanta, Georgia 30341
Telephone (404) 936-7511

April 13, 1977

Mr. Richard M. Wilson
General Manager
Financial Placement, Inc.
Post Office Box 3796
Memphis, Tennessee 38101

Dear Mr. Wilson:

Confirming our telephone conversation yesterday, I enclose my personal resume.

As we discussed, I am seeking a position as controller of a firm grossing in excess of $10 million annually, or as treasurer of a smaller company. I have a definite preference for a large city in the Southeast. My minimum salary requirement is $25,000. You may use this figure for your own reference, but I prefer that salary not be discussed with a potential employer.

As you will see in my resume, I have a broad background in financial management, with a history of implementing controls which increased profits. The four companies for which I have worked were all in different industries. This has exposed me to a wide variety of problems and methods of solution. I have also worked with many types of computers and computer access.

I would appreciate your sending my resume to any firms which retain you to fill appropriate vacancies and your advising me of their names. Because I am conducting a broad search on my own, I do not want my resume sent to firms which do not have a specific job opening. I will keep you advised of my availability.

Thank you for your kind assistance.

Yours truly,

William G. Naff

Enclosure

45

JERROLD A. BROOKS
1216 THORNHILL DRIVE
DALLAS, TEXAS 75221
TELEPHONE (214) 871-1496

February 5, 1977

Hoffman Associates
200 Fifth Avenue
Suite 1555
New York, New York 10017

Dear Sirs:

I have a 23-year career history with an apparel manufacturer that grew from $3.5 million to $25 million gross annual sales. During this period I served as vice-president or manager over marketing, merchandising, packaging, manufacturing, engineering, quality control, and purchasing.

Perhaps you know of a company that could use this scope of experience. In this regard, I enclose a copy of my resume outlining a few of my more significant accomplishments.

My objective is to find a position as vice-president of marketing or merchandising with a large company or as president or general manager of a smaller company or division. My preference would be to stay in an industry associated with apparel, textiles, or packaging.

I am not limited by location and would consider the challenge of complete responsibility over an unprofitable operation. My minimum salary requirement is in the $50,000 range and will depend upon location and potential. You may use this figure for your own reference. My preference is that you do not discuss salary with a potential employer.

Please advise me of any opportunities that I might investigate, or send my resume to companies that might be interested. Your assistance will be appreciated.

Yours truly,

Jerrold A. Brooks

Enclosure

SPECIAL SITUATION

DATE _____

Name of company _____

Headquarters address _____

City, state, zip code _____

Telephone number _____

Description of industry or industries _____
_____

Size of company: Annual gross sales _____
                 Number of employees _____

Type of company _____

Position desired _____

Responsibilities _____
_____

Location desired _____

Division or subsidiary if different from headquarters _____

Reasons for treating this as a special situation _____
_____
_____

Reasons you wish to work for this company _____
_____
_____

Reasons this company might hire you _____
_____
_____

Inside sources of information _____
_____

Outside sources of information _____
_____

Other contacts in a position to help _____
_____
_____
_____
_____

In regard to the author of the letter on the facing page, note his resume (#21) and his ad answer (#33). His effort with this local company was only one part of a job campaign that was national in scope.

Ronald J. Marque
Apartment 4, Terrace Court
Chicago, Illinois 47092
Telephone (312) 221-9130

April 21, 1977

Mr. Burnes G. Chardier
Vice-President, Finance
American Food Machinery, Inc.
Post Office Box 4000
Chicago, Illinois 47092

Dear Mr. Chardier:

I enjoyed meeting you last Monday and appreciate the preliminary interest you had in the possible use of regression analysis and econometric modeling for investment and other management decisions at American Food Machinery.

Following your suggestion, I set up a meeting with John Chandler on Monday of next week. I will use the information he gives me on past capital investments to perform several different decision analyses. I will compare these projected results with the actual current return. This will allow me to test my theory that such financial tools would be of benefit to American Food Machinery.

Then I will update the report I gave you. This should be completed by April 29. I will call you late next week to find a convenient time to discuss the results with you.

As you know, I am particularly interested in American Food Machinery and the possibility of joining your department as financial analyst. My report should demonstrate the contribution that I can make.

Thank you for your assistance.

Sincerely,

Ronald J. Marque

In regard to the author of the letter immediately following, note his ad response (#32). He had never been a manufacturer's representative but could phrase his accomplishments to give himself credibility in this field.

LEWIS B. SHOOKLER
365 Poinsettia Drive
Wilmington, Delaware 19804
Telephone (302) 879-6685

April 22, 1977

Mr. Lawrence Harbringer
Vice-President, Sales
Young Fashions, Inc.
714 Monte Verde Avenue
San Mateo, California 96074

Dear Mr. Harbringer:

I introduced a new career-apparel and lounge-wear line in Delaware, New Jersey, and Maryland, putting it into 71 accounts in less than two years.

Because you might need a manufacturer's representative with this kind of talent in all or a portion of these states, some of my other accomplishments might interest you.

--After taking over lines for an intimate-apparel company, I increased sales 48% in the first five months while adding 37 new accounts.
--I saw a potential new market and opened 11 military exchanges for a foundation line.
--In 17 years of territory sales experience in apparel, I have a continuous record of year-to-year volume increases and a far-above-average rapport with the key accounts in my region. I sell 90 of the 97 largest accounts in cities of 5,000 or more people.
--I worked with an outside consulting firm to develop a new merchandising program, which resulted in doubling department exposure for my lines in major accounts.

I am 43 years old, married, with five daughters ages 6 to 19. I travel my territory working out of a fully equipped mobile sales office. For new lines, I would expect a $100-per-week draw against a minimum 7% commission as well as an 80% delivery guarantee for commissions against firm orders.

I would welcome a personal meeting to discuss your line and the contribution I can make to your sales. I can be reached at the above number over the weekends or by message during the week after 3:00 P.M.

Yours truly,

Lewis B. Shookler

H. LEE RUST
3404 EAST BRIARCLIFF ROAD
BIRMINGHAM, ALABAMA 35223
TELEPHONE (205) 967-9728

January 14, 1977

Mr. Gerry Wiggers
President
Industrial Materials, Inc.
2222 South Fourth Avenue
Birmingham, Alabama 35210

Dear Mr. Wiggers:

I have a business associate and friend who is interested in purchasing all of or an equity position in an industrial supplies distributor or manufacturer's representative firm. Because this individual is now employed with a company you probably know, I must keep his name confidential until an interest in further discussions is established.

He is 35 years old and has a background in industrial engineering and construction with experience in industrial sales and purchasing. He is a native of Birmingham and is bright, aggressive, and one of the hardest workers that I know.

If you are interested in converting some of your years of work into equity, he may offer you such an opportunity. If you are interested in expanding your company, he can bring both capital and an additional, aggressive sales hand to your venture.

If you would like to discuss this possibility further, please call me at the above number after 5:00 P.M. or during the weekend. I might add that this letter is personal. I will not receive a commission or fee of any kind as a result of agreements you might reach.

Yours truly,

H. Lee Rust

William G. Naff
1674 North Park Drive
Atlanta, Georgia 30341
Telephone (404) 936-7511

April 5, 1977

Mr. Carlos Aslego
Vice-President, Finance
Morris Products Company
7514 Highway 31, South
Hapeville, Georgia 30354

Dear Mr. Aslego:

Confirming our telephone conversation yesterday, I will meet you at 10:30
A.M. on April 18 at the Morris Products plant.

I am most interested in the controller's position with your company and
look forward to discussing it with you and Mr. Wakefield.

Thank you for your consideration.

Yours truly,

William G. Naff

51

Ronald J. Marque
Apartment 4, Terrace Court
Chicago, Illinois 47092
Telephone (312) 221-9130

March 11, 1977

Mr. Charles G. Westmoreland
Industrial Products Manufacturing Company
Post Office Box 6713-A
Kansas City, Kansas 66117

Dear Mr. Westmoreland:

I want to confirm my interest in the financial analyst's position we discussed this morning.

Because most of your current investment decisions are based on paycheck period and return on investment only, I feel that I could contribute some new techniques that would give additional, useful data. The work I have done with business statistics and econometric modeling should also be applicable to analyzing new markets for Industrial Products Manufacturing Company.

In my last position I did an econometric model of residential housing demand and mortgage company competition in Chicago which showed a growing market segment attracting little attention from other firms. We used this information to sell over $25 million worth of loans.

After you have talked with other candidates, I would like to meet with you to discuss my background and the future plans of IPM in more detail. I will call you late this month to arrange a convenient time.

Thank you for your interest and consideration.

Cordially,

Ronald J. Marque

LEWIS B. SHOOKLER
365 Poinsettia Drive
Wilmington, Delaware 19804
Telephone (302) 879-6685

April 20, 1977

Mr. Wilson B. Myers
President
Merchandise Sales, Inc.
2712 South 20th Street
Hartford, Connecticut 06607

Dear Mr. Myers:

Thank you for your interest in me and my background. I was
impressed by the recent growth of your company and your description of
its future plans. Although I would like to participate in such an
aggressive organization, my intention is to remain in the Wilmington
area.

My current job search should be completed in another four weeks. If
I have not found a suitable position in Wilmington by then, I will call
you to arrange a meeting.

Meanwhile, I wish you the best of luck with your expansion plans.

Yours truly,

Lewis B. Shookler

CARTER M. HARLEN
3230 West Valley Drive
New Orleans, Louisiana 70132
Telephone (504) 977-8815

April 19, 1977

Mr. Brooks Stanford
Administrative Director
Crippled Children's Hospital
1900 Greenfield Avenue
New Orleans, Louisiana 70157

Dear Mr. Stanford:

Confirming our telephone conversation yesterday, I am most interested in
the planning and development position we discussed. Although you hope to
find a candidate with direct hospital experience, if you do not, I would
like to be considered.

My fund-raising experience with educational institutions should be
readily transferable to your hospital building program. In addition, my
business and construction background would also be of use.

I will plan to call you in about a month to check on your progress in
filling the position. Meanwhile, if you wish to talk with me further, I
will be available at your convenience.

Thank you for your kind consideration.

Sincerely,

Carter M. Harlen

MAILGRAM   MAILGRAM   MAILGRAM   MAILGRAM

Mr. Ladd D. Morris
Lansom Industries
2904 Wisconsin Avenue
Milwaukee, Wisconsin 65308

I have been unable to reach you since my letter of August 30 but am most interested in the position we discussed. Would you please call me when convenient at (205) 974-1396?

Ms. Joyce C. Barington

MAILGRAM   MAILGRAM   MAILGRAM   MAILGRAM

INTERVIEW QUESTIONS TO EXPECT

1. Did you bring a resume?
2. What salary do you expect to receive?
3. What was your salary in your last job?
4. Why do you want to change jobs or why did you leave your last job?
5. What do you identify as your most significant accomplishment in your last job?
6. How many hours do you normally work per week?
7. What did you like and dislike about your last job?
8. How did you get along with your superiors and subordinates?
9. Can you be demanding of your subordinates?
10. How would you evaluate the company you were with last?
11. What were its competitive strengths and weaknesses?
12. What best qualifies you for the available position?
13. How long will it take you to start making a significant contribution?
14. How do you feel about our company — its size, industry, and competitive position?
15. What interests you most about the available position?
16. How would you structure this job or organize your department?
17. What control or financial data would you want and why?
18. How would you establish your primary inside and outside lines of communication?
19. What would you like to tell me about yourself?
20. Were you a good student?
21. Have you kept up in your field? How?
22. What do you do in your spare time?
23. At what age do you want to retire?
24. What are your greatest strengths and weaknesses?
25. What is your job potential?
26. What are your career goals?
27. Do you want to own your own business?
28. How long will you stay with us?
29. What did your father do? Your mother?
30. What do your brothers and sisters do?
31. Are you a church member? Do you attend regularly?
32. Do you participate in civic affairs?
33. What professional associations do you belong to?
34. What is your credit standing?
35. What are your personal likes and dislikes?
36. How many children do you have?
37. Would you describe your family as a close one?
38. How aggressive are you?

39. What motivates you to work?
40. Is money a strong incentive for you?
41. Do you prefer line or staff work?
42. Would you rather work alone or in a team?
43. What do you look for when hiring people?
44. Have you ever fired anyone?
45. Can you get along with union members and their leaders?
46. What do you think of the current economic and political situation?
47. How will government policy effect our industry or your job?
48. Will you sign a noncompete agreement or employment contract?
49. Why should we hire you?
50. Do you want the job?
51. _____
52. _____
53. _____
54. _____
55. _____
56. _____
57. _____
58. _____
59. _____
60. _____
61. _____
62. _____
63. _____
64. _____
65. _____
66. _____
67. _____
68. _____
69. _____
70. _____

INTERVIEW QUESTIONS TO ASK

1. What is the first problem that needs the attention of the person you hire?
2. What other problems need attention now?
3. What has been done about any of these to date?
4. How has this job been performed in the past?
5. Why is it now vacant?
6. Do you have a written job description for this position?
7. What are its major responsibilities?
8. What authority would I have? How would you define its scope?
9. What are the company's five-year sales and profit projections?
10. What needs to be done to reach these projections?
11. What are the company's major strengths and weaknesses?
12. What are its strengths and weaknesses in production?
13. What are its strengths and weaknesses in its products or its competitive position?
14. Whom do you identify as your major competitors?
15. What are their strengths and weaknesses?
16. How do you view the future for your industry?
17. Do you have any plans for new products or acquisitions?
18. Might this company be sold or acquired?
19. What is the company's current financial strength?
20. What can you tell me about the individual to whom I would report?
21. What can you tell me about other persons in key positions?
22. What can you tell me about the subordinates I would have?
23. How would you define your management philosophy?
24. Are employees afforded an opportunity for continuing education?
25. What are you looking for in the person who will fill this job?
26. _____
27. _____
28. _____
29. _____
30. _____
31. _____
32. _____
33. _____
34. _____
35. _____

57

INTERVIEW RECORD

Company _____ Date _____

Contact's name _____

Title _____

Address _____ Phone _____

Products _____

Gross annual sales _____ Profits _____

Past five years sales growth _____% Past five years profits growth _____%

Number of employees _____ Years in business _____

Title of position discussed _____

Responsibilities _____

Questions:

_____
_____
_____
_____
_____
_____
_____
_____
_____
                                                                  *
_____
_____
_____
_____
_____
_____
_____
_____
_____

General impressions of interview _____
_____
_____
_____

Follow-up _____
_____

JERROLD A. BROOKS
1216 THORNHILL DRIVE
DALLAS, TEXAS 75221
TELEPHONE (214) 871-1496

February 28, 1977

Mr. Conway M. Green
President
Martex, Inc.
Post Office Box 740
Greenville, North Carolina 27601

Dear Conway:

I enjoyed our discussion this week. You have done an impressive job
with Martex including your five-year expansion plans.

I would like to participate in this next phase of your growth. My
merchandising experience during Howard & Sharpe's expansion years has
given me the background to anticipate some of the problems your firm
might face. As you know, I put Howard & Sharpe into perma press,
creating a new $2-million market. I also designed its plans to enter the
discount chain market. Evaluating the Martex line and identifying new
markets would be an attractive challenge.

I look forward to our next discussion at the New York fall show. As
soon as I arrive I will call your hotel to set a lunch date.

Sincerely,

Jerrold A. Brooks

R. Felix Thomason
1921 Forest Run Drive
Great Falls, Virginia 23322
Telephone (703) 775-6421

April 15, 1977

Mr. Martin B. Fairchild
President
Techmark Controls, Inc.
Post Office Box 179
Greenwich, Connecticut 04703

Dear Martin:

I enjoyed meeting you and Sam Burtcher this week and appreciate the job
offer you extended to me. It is attractive; the job is challenging.

My understanding is that the position of Vice-President, International
would carry a base salary of $40,000 per year with an incentive bonus to
be worked out mutually after the first year of operation. It will be
based on a percentage of before-tax profits generated by overseas sales.
An automobile, moving expenses, and two trips to the United States per
year for my family are included in addition to Techmark's standard
benefit package.

I will discuss this move with my wife, complete my investigation of one
other pending prospect, and get back in touch with you by April 27.

Thank you again for the confidence you have shown in me.

Yours truly,

R. Felix Thomason

JERROLD A. BROOKS
1216 THORNHILL DRIVE
DALLAS, TEXAS 75221
TELEPHONE (214) 871-1496

March 9, 1977

Mr. Richard A. Graffner, Jr.
President
Liberty Tailored Wear, Inc.
Post Office Box 19711
New York, New York 10022

Dear Dick:

Our meeting last week was a pleasure even though we could not reach agreement on my joining your company. Liberty Tailored Wear is an interesting firm. You have assembled an impressive group of executives.

If you are unsuccessful in finding an executive who meets your requirements for Vice-President of Marketing at your price, I would like to discuss this position again. Although my salary requirements may appear high, I can make a commensurate contribution to Liberty.

Thank you again for your kind consideration.

Cordially,

Jerrold A. Brooks

61

JERROLD A. BROOKS
1216 THORNHILL DRIVE
DALLAS, TEXAS 75221
TELEPHONE (214) 871-1496

March 14, 1977

Mr. Conway M. Green
President
Martex, Inc.
Post Office Box 740
Greenville, North Carolina 27601

Dear Conway:

My wife and I appreciate the dinner you arranged for us. Meeting your wife and the wives of your associates was also an unexpected pleasure.

I look forward to receiving your offer next week. I am most interested in the position with Martex.

You will hear from me prior to the end of the month. Meanwhile, I send my best regards.

Yours truly,

Jerrold A. Brooks

62

RECORD OF JOB OFFER

DATE _____

Company _____
Contact and title _____
Address _____
_____ Telephone _____

Position _____
Responsibilities _____
_____

Location _____

Starting salary _____

Benefits:	Comments	Value
Vacations		
Holidays		
Group insurance, hospital		
Life		
Accident		
Major medical		
Disability		
Dental		
Sick leave		
Automobile		
Expense account		
Pension		
Bonus		
Stock options		
Other		

Total value, salary and benefits _____

Comments on moving expenses and other items _____
_____
_____
_____
_____

63

EVALUATION OF JOB OFFERS

NAME _____   DATE _____

Item	I	II	III	IV
Position				
Title				
Responsibilities				
Authority				
Industry				
Company, size and type				
Company, style and character				
Location				
Salary				
Benefits				
Promotion potential				
Salary potential				
Equity potential				
Work hours				
Travel				
Security				
Challenge				
Professional risk				
Variety and interest				
Contacts with--People				
--Data				
--Things				
Personal relationships				
Internal politics				
Recognition--Professional				
--Civic				
--Personal				
Contribution to career goals				
Spouse's preference				
Overall preference				

R. Felix Thomason
1921 Forest Run Drive
Great Falls, Virginia 23322
Telephone (703) 775-6421

April 28, 1977

Mr. Martin B. Fairchild
President
Techmark Controls, Inc.
Post Office Box 179
Greenwich, Connecticut 04703

Dear Martin:

Confirming our telephone conversation yesterday, I wish to accept the
position of Vice-President, International with Techmark Controls. The
conditions of employment are as outlined in my letter of April 15, 1977,
except for the addition of an overseas housing allowance of $200 per
month.

I will report to your Greenwich office on May 16 and will be ready to
leave for Brussels with my family on June 15.

I am looking forward to working with you and your associates. The
position is an attractive opportunity and challenge.

Yours truly,

R. Felix Thomason

R. Felix Thomason
1921 Forest Run Drive
Great Falls, Virginia 23322
Telephone (703) 775-6421

April 28, 1977

Mr. Fred M. Langford
President
Overseas Oil, Inc.
Post Office Box 6000
Houston, Texas 77025

Dear Fred:

I have accepted the position of Vice-President, International with Techmark Controls. Although I was strongly interested in the position with Overseas Oil, I felt I could better use my industrial and sales experience in the process controls industry.

I want to thank you and your associates for your offer and your kind consideration.

Yours truly,

R. Felix Thomason

William G. Naff
1674 North Park Drive
Atlanta, Georgia 30341
Telephone (404) 936-7511

April 27, 1977

Mr. K. R. Greenfield
Manager
Compushare, Inc.
2117 First Avenue, North
Atlanta, Georgia 30308

Dear Kirk:

I have just accepted the position of controller with Morris Products in Hapeville. Your assistance and excellent reference for me helped make this move possible.

If I can ever reciprocate, please call me.

Thank you again. Drop in to see me on your next visit to Hapeville.

Cordially,

William G. Naff

INDEX